SANTA FE

SANTA FE

Santa Fe

GENERAL MOTOR

D1261542

THE Super CHIEF
...Train of the Stars

Stan Repp

Golden West Books
· San Marino, California ·

SUPER CHIEF: Train of the Stars

Copyright © 1980 by Stan Repp

All Rights Reserved
Published by Golden West Books
San Marino, California 91108 U.S.A.

Library of Congress Catalog Card No. 80-18725
I.S.B.N. 0-87095-081-9

Library of Congress Cataloging in Publication Data

Repp, Stan, 1919–
    The Super Chief, train of the stars.

    Includes indexes.
    1. Super Chief (Express train) 2. Atchison,
Topeka and Santa Fe Railway. I. Title.
TF25.A7R46   385′.37′0978   80-18725

TITLE PAGE ILLUSTRATION

Its red-and-yellow nose bearing the first of two-thousand miles . . . steam leaking and hissing from lines in back of the pilot and under the engines . . . sand trailing out of the sander-cocks in tan billows . . . fumes spewing upward in sparking plumes from a final gunning of the Diesels . . . two brief snorts of the air horn and *Super Chief-2* — digging its "heels" into the track like a cowpoke bull-dogging a steer — shouldered its hot, oily bulk through a waiting crowd strewn around La Grande Station on her first arrival in Los Angeles, May 10, 1937.

Raymond Spencer's vigorous and vivid painting enables us to re-live that Super moment!

Golden West Books

P.O. BOX 8136 • SAN MARINO, CALIFORNIA • 91108

JULIE STECKEL made this book happen.
Without her, it would not, could not
have been written.

The booklet, announcing the inaugural running of the new *Super Chief,* was a bright spot of 1936 printing art. This conception of the train's new Diesel locomotives appeared on the title page. — DONALD DUKE COLLECTION

Before Beginning

I n a 10x11-inch, brownish colored booklet put out in early May of 1936, the Santa Fe Railway presented its brand new, heavyweight, Diesel-drawn *Super Chief* thusly. We quote:

"PRESENTING ... THE NEW SUPER CHIEF
Proudly this train of trains ... the Santa Fe's new *Super Chief* ... glides quietly out of the station, imperceptibly picks up speed, and streaks off on its regular once-a-week run between Chicago and Los Angeles ... and from the west coast, back. Newest of a long line of fine and famous trains ... the *Super Chief* epitomizes luxurious, modern train travel. Perfectly appointed ... swift and smooth as the flight of an arrow ... less than forty hours *en route* ... a super-schedule.

Before you board the *Super Chief,* walk down to see the mighty, powerful Diesel locomotive, designed especially to pull this swift new transcontinental flyer. Thirty-six hundred H.P. under perfect control ... a sweeping, clean length of over one hundred and twenty-seven feet ... a triumph of modern engineering.

Notice the operator's cab and control station ... the clear, unobstructed view ahead and at both sides. Here is

This large brochure introduced the new *Super Chief* to agents and the riding public. Of special interest was the reduction of 14 hours from the regular schedule, an extra-fare of $10, and the twin-unit Diesel locomotives. Announced was the weekly round trip schedule, the handpicked

mechanical efficiency, safety and power. Here's a modern travel thrill ... only one business day between Chicago and California.

Though the primary purpose of the new *Super Chief* is to save hours of time between Chicago and the Coast ... the fast record schedule is accomplished with no sacrifice of comfort ... no compromise with luxury. From the powerful Diesel ... back through each of its beautifully appointed cars ... the passenger's pleasure and comfort are paramount.

Wide aisles ... full length berths ... roomy compartments and drawing rooms ... spacious lounge sections ... all contribute to one's physical well-being. Completely air-conditioned cars assure properly controlled temperature at all times ... as well as the knowledge that no dust, wrinkles or rumples will mar one's appearance at the end of the trip.

And through its windows ... streaking by in time to the tick of the minute hand ... valleys, mesas, high, majestic mountains; wide sweeping plains, prosperous farms and ranches; red-gold soil, sage-green cacti; turquoise skies ... magnificent vistas of color and contrast.

There is but one Santa Fe Train ... the pathway to the west which has woven its glamorous pattern through the

personnel and that the train would consist of the finest standard equipment until an entirely new train of lightweight stainless steel cars arrived. The first sailing was scheduled for May 12, 1936, and all cars would be air-conditioned. — MERRILL COLLECTION

pages of American history. There is but one *Super Chief* . . . the Santa Fe train that's writing a new page in the history of fast, luxurious western travel.

Every effort is made aboard the *Super Chief* to provide the fullest measure of service . . . typical Santa Fe attention and courtesy. The entire staff . . . steward, waiters, porters, maid and barber-valet have been trained in the best traditions of this famous transcontinental railroad. The very atmosphere of the *Super Chief* has the charm and dignity of a well-run home. The Fred Harvey food is world-famous.

Truly, here is comfort spelled with well-bred restraint and flawless good taste . . . a distinctive train for those fastidious men and women who expect and demand the finest in travel.

Only one business day between Chicago and Los Angeles on

THE SUPER CHIEF

39 ¾ HOURS CHICAGO–CALIFORNIA

Ten Dollars Extra-Fare

That was Santa Fe's first *Super* credo, a vigorous and glowing promise to its ridership. We now examine how that promise was manifested, how the *Super Chief* became an institution.

9

The maiden run of the new *Super Chief* in May of 1936, depicted here as it rolls down the west side of Cajon Pass between Victorville and San Bernardino, was made with all-Pullman standard equipment behind Diesel-electric units Nos. 1 and 1-A. New motive power was procured in April of the following year and streamlined equipment was integrated into the schedule. — DEGOLYER FOUNDATION LIBRARY

Table of Contents

Newspaper advertisements announcing the new *Super Chief* appeared in many metropolitan newspapers, such as this art piece published in the *New York Times* on April 28, 1936.

Foreword

That admirably facile writer, David Morgan, Editor of *Trains,* once said, "Santa Fe made the most of the prefix 'super.' In a sense, the road's publicists had little choice; they had already employed such ultimates as *De Luxe, Saint, Angel,* and *Chief.* When the road diesel showed up in 1936 and promised to squeeze those 2222.7 miles between Chicago and Los Angeles into an unprecedented 39 hours 45 minutes—a super schedule calling for a supertrain—there was no name for that train but *Super Chief.*"

When all was said and done, *The Super Chief* was super, because, right off the bat, it was familiar; familiar in the most unique, most desirable sense of the word.

The bulk of its passengers had, for years, travelled in the *Chief* ... *Chief,* old-line family-retainer, trusted, predictable, devoted, symbol of the Santa Fe. The *Chief* had accustomed its patrons to its staff, its atmosphere, its route, its cuisine, even its regular riders. It wasn't difficult, therefore, to understand the ease with which the *Chief* riders so easily, so naturally, so quickly, so eagerly took to a *Chief* with "Super" tucked in front.

Santa Fe, as any firm of transport should, valued, nay treasured, the familiarity factor ... the selling point of happy habit or, in other words, whatever its customers were used to if, of course, it was "good, better, or best" that they were used to. And, surely, their Premier Train should, they reasoned, be, first and foremost, familiar. That's why their entry into the era of streamlining was not likened to bullets, rockets, zephyrs, or any other pseudonyms for trajectory, propulsion, or atmospheric disturbance.

Santa Fe, quite wisely, clung, familialy, to a household name, *Chief,* and claimed, with understandable parentalism, that it was SUPER.

The Super's Hollywood-Broadway-Commerce passengers rode it often and regularly. For that matter, they rode anything often and regularly. Accordingly, like so many nomads, they sought to reduce the effects of their enforced transiency whenever they could and, thus, rather appreciated an aura of permanency when they did alight. Their contractual wanderings caused them to yearn for a place, any place, to settle down—even if that place was in-motion. And, if that in-motion place was a familiar one, so much the better.

The trip aboard *The Super Chief,* unlike shorter, overnight train journeys, provided the show-and-business folk with nearly forty hours of settlement; time for permanency of sorts to be ensconced happily in its berths, rooms, and other accommodations of range and note. Forty hours of time to become attached to their *Super Chief.* They could, truly, kick off their shoes and be at-home.

Of that *Super* train, this writer, obviously a *devotée* of its superness, has long believed that the ramifications of its creation, construction, inauguration, and eminence deserved telling and, in that story process, the chronicling of a bright facet of American transport. Moreover, from the standpoint of rail history alone, if that isn't too lofty a categorizing, *The Super Chief* occupied a highly prominent segment of that history and, thus additionally, rates display.

Then, too, as fortune would have it, *The Super Chief* was THE train which, when most people were asked to name one, they mentioned first.

The first *Super Chief* was far from *le dernier cri* in trains but it was still infinitely more than a mechanical entity, more than six refurbished, heavyweight cars rolling, solitarily, between Chicago and Los Angeles—once a week. For one thing, her sleeping cars inspired affection. William Rose Benet rhymed about her . . .

"Green aisles of her Pullmans soothe me like trees, woven in old tapestries." Another of her first passengers, sculptor Julie Petit-Malin, in a practical but no less poetical vein, said . . . "Her level orbit, the path she trod so debonairly, her passionate speed hurled me on my way with relentless sureness—*le train magnifique.*" Ballet dancer Margaret Lois Young recollected delightedly after more than four decades . . . "I used to love to sit in my berth on *The Super,* at night, and with my knees drawn up under by chin, rock to the motion of the train, watching the desert whiz past my window. *The Super* was my rhythmic pause in time."

This sprinkling of affectionate conjuring up of the first *Super Chief* says, rather graphically, that the six old cars made conquests that have lasted, lo, these many years.

As a matter of fact, rare, indeed, is the Hollywood or Broadway personality who, when the name *Super Chief* is brought up, doesn't have an anecdote to tell about a ride, or rides, on the train. *The Super,* for some reason, inspires almost total recall on the parts of its passengers. In most cases, they can recite the date—at least the year—and, invariably, the occasion why they were on board, who else was riding, what they had to eat, the steward's name, quite often the number of their bedroom or drawing room and, without fail, what cards they held in a poker session! *The Super* made "pitchers" of people in that, like baseball hurlers, they could dredge-up, instantly, the precise "pitch" they threw for that "homerun" forty years ago.

Just for a moment, let's pedanticize and, in our introduction of *The Super Chief,* examine, briefly, three phases of *Super Chiefery.* First of all, *The Super* schedule was speedy but, then, so was the Union Pacific's "City of Los Angeles," which made it between Chicago and the Coast in the same 39 hours 45 minutes. Secondly, *The Super* was luxurious but, again, so was the "City"— maybe not as elegantly luxurious but, all the same, luxurious. Thirdly, of course, *Super* cuisine was *hâute* but, there again, one could also dine expansively aboard U.P.'s "City."

So, as one goes down the list of its strong points, *The Super's* superness, it would seem, is diminished by comparison with a train that was its only "competitor." No, not really, for by cancelling-out what people have long taken for granted as its own special features, we do, oddly enough, get at the heart of *The Super* matter . . . what it was that really put Santa Fe's best at the top of the heap. We discover that its appeal, its enormous appeal, was tangibly intangible: to wit, when viewed most objectively, *The Super* was an extension of long-time *Chief* familiarity and, perhaps more than anything in its favor, permitted Hollywood-Broadway *habitués* to say six words that they delighted in saying ... "just got in on the Super."

Riding *The Super* was belonging, being "in," having status, club, and class. Its *Super* name was one to pronounce "trippingly" on the tongue, a name to reckon with, a name to inspire envy or, better still, camaraderie in the one to whom it was mentioned.

The Super Chief came on the train-scene known, liked, and of reliable lineage, the brightest star in Santa Fe's firmament. Here's how it was done.

Stan Repp

Manhattan Beach
January 3, 1980

THE Super CHIEF

Eleanor Powell, Hollywood's legendary dancer, waves farewell to Chicago from the *Super Chief* on its maiden departure from Dearborn Station, May 12, 1936. "Ellie," its first passenger, set the pattern for *Super's* elegant show-business clientele and no one deserves more than she does to be identified with Santa Fe's *Train of the Stars*.

The first Diesel-electric locomotives, Nos. 1 and 1-A on the Santa Fe's first *Super Chief,* as photographed at Dearborn Station on May 12, 1936, on the maiden run. Engineer Manley Marsh, who ran the units from Chicago to Fort Madison, waves from the cab window. — SANTA FE RAILWAY

1

It was six-fifteen, Tuesday evening, May 12th, 1936 in the looming darkness of the train shed at Chicago's time-worn Dearborn Station. At the end of Track 5, the red and white letters S-u-p-e-r-C-h-i-e-f glowed softly on the glass face of a lighted, circular purple sign gracing the brass railing of a heavy Pullman observation car—a railing barely visible under a blanket of fragrant fresh-cut spring flowers.

Escaping steam vapor rose lazily out of a coupling-hose to cast intermittent wispy veils over the richly-colored blossoms framing the red Indian-head insignia and white Santa Fe emblem which also adorned the lighted round of purple.

Off to one side of Track 5, a gaudily uniformed band was blaring-out Sousa favorites while sweating red caps scurried, luggage-laden, along a stretch of red carpet out to four gleaming Pullmans.

Up on the observation platform, blinking at popping flash bulbs, WGN Announcer Truman Bradley beamed a fifteen-minute "remote" broadcast interviewing celebrities such as Ida Cantor and daughters and new film star—tap dancer Eleanor Powell, all of it to the delight of a crowd pressed against the gated area in back of Track 5.

Samuel T. Bledsoe, president of the Santa Fe Railway, speaking at the ceremonies just before the new *Super Chief* left for Los Angeles on its first run.

Mrs. Eddie Cantor and two daughters on the rear platform of the *Super Chief*. The gentleman is WGN announcer, Truman Bradley.

Mrs. Bartlett Cormack, daughter of President Samuel T. Bledsoe of the Santa Fe, prepares to christen the new *Super Chief* with a ribboned bottle of the best California Champagne.

If ever an "air of expectancy" pervaded a place, it did that May night at Dearborn where, amidst more splash and splendor than the old depot had seen since the turn of the century, Santa Fe was celebrating a triple *fête:* the birth of its very first *Super Chief,* its President, Samuel Bledsoe, and his daughter, Adelaide Cormack, and, it must be said, doing itself proud in the bargain.

Even upstairs, on the mezzanine, from a big plate glass window overlooking the train gates, hundreds pushed against that glass to catch every bit of the action below. The din of chatter grew by the minute; suspense heightened.

At the stroke of "7:15," with the crowd and the band pretty well played-out, Mrs. Cormack—timorously clutching a yellow-ribboned bottle of California Champagne—stepped to the railing and, just as Engineer Manley Marsh feather-eased six cars out into the near darkness and the band struck up "California Here I Come," she smashed the bottle into the bed of flowers, sending bubbles spilling in a fizzing trail along the greasy track leading out of Dearborn depot.

As the band played *California Here I Come,* the new *Super Chief* departs Dearborn Station, the dignitaries wave farewell. Left to right, President Bledsoe, Mrs. Eddie Cantor, Mrs. Bartlett Cormack, Eleanor Powell and Mrs. Samuel Bledsoe.

Cheers went up. The band finished strong. The "celebs" waved from the observation platform and a fast-fading purple sign and red tail lights were all that marked the christening ceremony of seconds past.

Still trailing flower petals as it rounded the curve south of Roosevelt Road, *The Super Chief* was, at last, on the timecard and in-business: a rolling six-car, Diesel-drawn advertisement—day-in, day-out—carrying *The Super Chief* insignia and the Santa Fe herald up and down the system ... most importantly, into the outskirts of Hollywood presaging, as it were, to the film-set, their new magic carpet and eventual replacement of the cherished-and-clubby, nine-and-a-half-year-old *Chief.*

The telling of that christening and departure has, of course, been oversimplified, but the impact of it is still felt: *The Super Chief,* in its relatively brief life-span, achieved a reputation and stature that other named trains worked years longer to attain yet never quite realized.

Actually, *The Super* gained its enviable standing in the rail-community early in its career, but the passing years, like coats of varnish on a painting, only heightened its luster. Eminence of that sort and duration was not accidental. Five factors aided, vitally, *The Super's* rapid rise to the top:

1. From the beginning, thanks largely to the consistent patronage of the storied motion-picture people, *The Super Chief* enjoyed extraordinary "press" even though much of that coverage—wrapped in crypticisms, couched in caprices, or reduced to train-order dialogue—glossed over salient features of the train and highlighted, instead, the doings of its passengers. But, no matter, all the while the tastes and habits of its film-star and theatrical riders were becoming common knowledge, *The Super's* stock rose right along with the appearance of each news-story. Even Frederic Wakeman's salty prose about *Super* life in his book, "The Hucksters," kept the publicity pot boiling and, better still, *The Super's* name squarely in the public eye.

2. Beside the muscular assist from the Fourth Estate, *The Super* got a rousing boost from its famed predecessor, the *Chief*, which, for nine-and-a-half years, had gotten the Hollywood and Broadway crowds used to *Chief* trains, *Chief* food, *Chief* service, *Chief* right-of-way, and *Chief* stations. When the *Super Chief* went into service, all the "regulars" had to do was step off the *Chief* and onto *The Super Chief*. For theatre and movie people, going *Super Chief* was going home.

3. An astounding amount of unsolicited advertising ranging from spot mentions on radio to detailed model-trains gave *The Super Chief* a familiarity-rating and writeaboutability unmatched by anything else hauling passengers.

4. For the manifestly short-tempered of its clientele, eager to catch *The Century* or *The Broadway* for "Lindy's" and the "Big Apple," *The Super Chief* required but one-business-day to haul its tinselled and luxuriously-luggaged time-watchers between Hollywood and Chicago. In 1936, when airplanes carried, at most, 23 passengers and took, at best, 12 hours for the same journey, *The Super's* one-business-day wasn't all *that* much longer. Indeed, it was, all things considered, a pretty respectably competitive schedule.

5. For the publicity-shy producers, directors and moguls-in-general, *The Super* provided, perhaps, its most saleable commodity ... *privacy!* Privacy to eat and drink (maybe *over*eat and *over*drink), chase secretaries, create stars, make deals, study scripts, hob-nob with other moguls ... and do it all in the im-

mured, sequestered company of those of equal rank and redoubtable notability.

Quickly reviewing, *The Super Chief* and its forerunner, the *Chief,* offered these attractive features that their principal competition, the airplane, could not and still does not offer:

—a familiar rolling sanctuary, hide-out, or club
—a sequestered sleeping, eating, drinking place
—a respite from devilments and pressures; privacy
—an "in" showplace for egoism and camaraderie
—a pause in time to resuscitate the mind and body

Granted, then, *The Super Chief* was club-and-class wrapped in stainless steel, whizzing its pampered payloads along behind garishly-colored, bluntnosed Diesels, setting them down at either terminal without so much as a hair out of place.

Say what you will, Santa Fe, with its Depression-born *Super Chief,* had a corner on the market of chic-and-client and, already, a submission hold on its neighbor railroads ... a hold that, until years later when jet engines all but cleared the rails, they would never relinquish.

Super Chiefing was, in those gentler and vastly less involved days before World War II, realistically or not, the *only way to go!*

—*Super* CHIEF

Regrettably, the bulk of the writing on, the publicity about, and the photographing of *The Super Chief* was done during its first years. Consequently, few (astonishingly few) people know how *The Super* began, why it was released in two stages, where and when the elegantly colorful first streamlined model was built, and what the conditions were that brought about its creation in the first place. So, suppose we go back through the years and explore discoverable areas of *The Super Chief* tradition.

As much as those of analytical bent might wish that they were, many fine points of early *Super Chiefery* are simply not available. The precise conceptual processes of *The Super Chief* are so clouded in vagaries and elapsed time that it's just not feasible to attempt their exposure.

In 40 years, people and records and trains and even places disappear. Cost-reports, contracts, inventories, performance charts, wine lists, menus, timetables, brochures, passenger-lists and, most tragically, photographs are, except in rare instances, gone

... fallen prey to a management syndrome called "making way for new records." *Super Chief* passenger-lists, had its owners seen fit to keep them, would read like "Who's Who" and offer-up pages of legendary names of the arts and, more specifically, show business!

It remains, then, for us, its devoted, string-saving, uncompanied contemporaries, to recollect, dig into, and lay before today's readers *Super Chief* treasures, in the doing of it, wracking happy, though sometimes recalcitrant brains for memories and descriptions of a great train in great times.

Parenthetically, even when one can find oldtimers who were in on the start of *The Super Chief*, their stories vary widely (sometimes heatedly) as to precisely what *did* happen "way back when." What's more, a peculiar kind of possessiveness takes hold of the oldsters when they reminisce about *their* departments. Diesel maintainers belittle enginemen, traffic men scoff at operating people, dining car men grumble about maintenance-of-way crews, each to his own, as it were.

But, the fact remains, allegiances notwithstanding, the listing of *Super Chief* progenitors can and does go on and on and on. Dipping into the welter of those who were "in" when the "cards were dealt" at Santa Fe and Electro-Motive, we find names such as Birdseye, Black, Bledsoe, Brasher, Dilworth, Ellis, Etter, Gill, Goodrich, Gurley, Knickerbocker, Kuehn, Lanning, McDonald, Milton, Morris, Purcell, Ripley, Tausch ... and more.

At best, then, what millions knew as *The Super Chief* stands most compatibly revealed as a many-faceted gem, intriguing but not to be too searchingly geologized. Suffice to say, for the first five years of its life, the time it epitomized and glorified the term all-Pullman, *The Super Chief* ranked as a simon-pure American institution ... an inordinately writeaboutable train for transporting the fabled and foibled in and out of Hollywood and the Babylons of commerce.

—*Super* CHIEF

In the early 1930's (bad times with a capital "B,") Santa Fe had more than its share of problems and things-to-do. Chief among them, according to Mechanical Officer E. E. Chapman, was to "drastically cut the running times of its Chicago–Los Angeles trains."

Planes, buses, automobiles and, most notably, neighboring railroads were waking-up, speeding-up, dressing-up, and luring travellers to them. Santa Fe's only alternative was to lure back and, in that regard, consider first how to set-up and maintain a schedule needing but ONE BUSINESS DAY to travel between its big terminals.

Ever since 1926 when they put on the *Chief,* Santa Fe and its peripatetic Hollywood-Broadway-Big Business clientele had dreamed of the one business day schedule to get the moguls and mahatmas back and forth from Chicago to Los Angeles in something like 40-hours. In the Twenties, however, Santa Fe's chances for a 40-hour system-run with its then-prime-mover—steam— were as remote as chamber music in the roundhouse. Defeated but not discouraged, Santa Fe kept right on dreaming, dreaming hard, too!

Acutely aware of steam's long-distance limitations, progressive thinkers in Santa Fe's engineering office had, over the years, been casting sidelong glances at the highways paralleling their tracks, watching the rapid development of automobiles and trucks and wondering, sequentially, as Lucius Beebe put it, "whether there would be any gain in the adaptation of the *internal combustion engine* to railroad propulsion."

Not altogether sure *how* it could be accomplished, Santa Fe's engineers, nonetheless, kept on calculating and conjuring, always visualizing *internal combustion* pulling their trains, most especially, that one business day flyer to the Coast.

Of course, in addition to their 40-hour "Grand Plan" and courting new motive-power, Santa Fe, as the Thirties bloomed, wore four other "hair shirts:" their parched desert right-of-way, their lack of good water, their obsolescing passenger cars, and their customers' desire to go faster.

At any rate, in those beginning Thirties, Santa Fe's thinking and motordom's logical development (largely the work of Harold Hamilton at Electro-Motive) led the road into gasoline motortrains for local runs. And, after Charlie Kettering whittled-down the enormity of Herr Diesel's earlier engines and tucked them into a body that *could* fit on rails, Santa Fe bought three 660-h.p. Diesel motor-cars, and its first Diesel switch engine in mid-1934 and, accordingly, got to know, first-hand, that remarkably versatile source of power, the Diesel.

Santa Fe, a steam railroad, was thus at the edge of the Diesel mainstream readied for baptism into the nitty-gritty of Thermal

Efficiency Ratios. Popularly stated, thermal efficiency is *a measure of an engine's ability to put-to-use the potential energy in a given amount of fuel!*

As of 1931– '32, steam engines had a thermal efficiency of 5–8 percent, gasoline engines: 20–25 percent, Diesel engines: 33–38 percent. Case stated; case closed! It wasn't hard to see, therefore, which power source would, from then on, be the "fair-haired boy" in Santa Fe's engine dreams and plans.

But, all the same, even though they were, at last, into Diesels, albeit small ones, Santa Fe—as they always had—still yearned for that BIG Diesel, the one that would go out on the road and haul its cherished transcontinental flyer.

All the fuss-and-feathers, here and abroad, in the early Thirties about streamlining, "bullet" designs, wind-tunnel testing, lightweight alloys, and "toy trains" (as Motive Power Chief John Purcell called the articulated units then skimming the rails) had not and would not dissuade Santa Fe from its set mode of thinking, although they were impressed with one thing, *lightweight alloy cars.*

Even a trip to Germany (1933) by one of their vice presidents, to sketch and ride a two-car speedster, *The Flying Hamburger,* did not influence the road's planning but, again, the lightweight cars were "notable." Santa Fe wanted and always had wanted a REAL engine and a REAL train. Specifically, an engine, or engines, that they could hook-up or hook-onto, or cut-out of a train comprised, most importantly, of separate cars, takeapartable components which were nothing at all like the articulated two and three-car, less-than-standard-gauge whippets in action as of 1933–'34.

To Santa Fe, an inordinately well-informed, *au courant* railroad that had done its homework, Reading and T & P motortrains, Union Pacific's "M-10000" and Burlington's "Zephyr" were no more surprises, innovations, or attractions than ham with eggs. They simply weren't what Santa Fe wanted!

In any event, with the tantalizing scent of REAL motive progress in its nostrils, and the crystalizing image of its "dream train" on the horizon, Santa Fe—early in 1934—began urging, in earnest, Hal Hamilton and Dick Dilworth, at GM's Electro-Motive plant, to put-together that BIG Diesel for them: something, say, around 3,600 h.p., a figure compatible with the speeds, weights, mileage, and geography of a 40-hour Chicago–LA run.

The hot and hazy summer of 1934 meandered by and saw endless conferences at Dilworth's office and Santa Fe's headquarters, the sweltering days hard on tempers and notepads. On September 19th, 1934, armed with papers and purpose, Santa Fe signed the order for its first road Diesel. The die was cast!

Oh, to be sure, beside engines, power-ratios, and schedules, Santa Fe, in '34 and '35, had other "fish to fry." With new power in the offing, new cars for more trains would have to be fashioned. Fashioning, though, would take time and, in Santa Fe's book, time was money, time was useful, and time was *now.*

Thus, it was more than just a speed-up that Santa Fe was after. They were out to save their WHOLE PASSENGER FLEET!

The plighting of its troth with Diesel, speedier and infinitely more workable power than Steam—actually an open sesame to an all-new future—dictated that Santa Fe perform total corrective surgery on its aging passenger fleet, even to creating, in the operation, three FULL trains—lightweight construction, of course—with three new names never before seen in their timetable. They totally re-equipped six trains of that pricelessly-patronized Hollywood-favorite, the seven-and-a-half-year-old rolling "Hillcrest Country Club," the *Chief.*

Before new trains were begun, however, Santa Fe—as was typical of the road's 1930's wisdom—wanted just one of those *big* lightweight cars to run and test, but it had to be "full-conventional width, height, and length," something that had not, as of 1934, been built (*Zephyr* and UP *Streamliner* cars were not "full size" cars).

So, to serve as a forerunner for all the lightweight cars they envisioned in their fleet-surgery, Santa Fe turned to *the* pioneer lightweight trainmakers, the Edward G. Budd Manufacturing Company (hereinafter called the Budd Company) in Philadelphia, and ordered one stainless steel day coach for in-train testing and a good look-see.

Imagine, all that in the depths of The Depression. There, in awesomely grim times, in one fell swoop of planning, Santa Fe would conceive *two* less-than-forty-hour, Diesel-drawn Chicago-to-Los Angeles trains:

1. America's first all-Pullman Diesel-consist, a 9-car "SUPER" *Chief.*

2. An all-Coach companion, the 6-car *El Capitan.*

28

In appearance the new loco... even in this day of strangely ga... of the grim and still highly effici...

A pleasing effect of streamlinin... tained for the twin units by skillfu... in the steel jackets that hide ev... engineering apparatus; by the r... slope of the rather blunt ends; the f... "skirts", with removable sections, tha... wheels and underbody, and the skillfu... of an attractive color scheme in black, c... sarasota blues, golden olive and pimper... let, worked out by the Art and Color Dep... of the General Motors Corporation, of wh... Electro-Motive Corporation is a subsidiary... effect is heightened by an unusual applicati... the familiar Santa Fe emblem of a maltese c... in a circle, combined with the strong slop... head and streaming headdress of an Indian chi... that has long been used by the road in its adve...

A MIGHTY
DIESEL
LOCOMOTIVE
designed to draw the
NEW
Super CHIEF

...e Santa Fe has ...resting engines ...tive worthy of ...e Super-Chief.

...d grueling ...nteresting ...hed east- ...minutes, ...tbound, ...impres- ...to Los

...ges; ...er longer dis- ...asioned by operating checks, ...ted for water and fuel stops, locomotive ...d engine changes.

tising. These emblems, in full color and nearly eight feet long, take the place of the old matter-of-fact letters of identification. They are not painted on the sides of the engine units, but were first drawn on heavy steel plates, enameled, baked, and then riveted home. The name "Super CHIEF", chosen for the train the big Diesel eventually is to draw, has been etched on heavy glass panels, electrically lighted, and let into the end of the locomotive between the forward windows of the driving cabs.

The Santa Fe published this brochure extolling the virtues of this new means of railroad locomotion designed to draw the new *Super Chief*.
—DONALD DUKE COLLECTION

Allies
FOR BETTER
SERVICE

The Super Chief, latest development in high-speed Diesel-powered locomotives is being placed in service by the Santa Fe primarily for the purpose of maintaining the high standard of service for which *The Chief*, only remaining extra fare train between Chicago and the Pacific Coast, is rightfully famous. It is quite fitting, therefore, that Winton-Diesel engines were selected to power this outstanding locomotive, because the paramount aim of Winton engineers is to incorporate in Winton-Diesel Engines only such engineering advances as promote improved standards of service and operating efficiency. Truly a worthy combination working together in the new era of railroading.

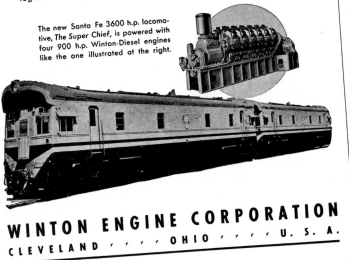

The new Santa Fe 3600 h.p. locomotive, *The Super Chief*, is powered with four 900 h.p. Winton-Diesel engines like the one illustrated at the right.

WINTON ENGINE CORPORATION
CLEVELAND ⟩ ⟩ ⟩ OHIO ⟩ ⟩ ⟩ U. S. A.

Suppliers of railroad parts and equipment were quick to jump on the band wagon concerning this radical change in motive power. The Winton Engine Corporation, builder of the unit's power plant, placed this ad in *Railway Age,* a trade publication. — A. E. BARKER COLLECTION

And, if that wasn't enough, a 6-car *San Diegan* was slated to flash over the 126 miles between the "Silver City" and LA.

So it was, back in the winter of 1934, that Santa Fe's long-cherished dreams were, though not fully realized, at least in the works, tangible pieces of long-range projection. What with new engines and new cars foreseen, Santa Fe, then, had to make a snow-soft path for its soon-to-be-born, shiny-faced cars and their big growling locomotives that would, with one swift stroke, sever *14* and *15¼* hours from the fastest 1934 schedules!

For that anticipated robust rise in acceleration, it was evident, crackingly evident, that drastic improvement of tracks and signals was vital. Never before had the road's rails been made to withstand such high *sustained* speeds as the new *Super Chief* and its companions' schedules would dictate. This was to be a racing railroad and, for its race-course, Santa Fe was faced with a tab of better than 4½ million dollars, to be spent something like this: $1,827,000 for new 112-pound rail . . . $1,500,000 straightening curves . . . $700,000 superelevating curves and re-ballasting track . . . and $500,000 on signals.

That out-of-pocket spending is doubly significant nowadays when one can think back to the mid-Thirties and consider that receivership was a constant bedfellow of most of Santa Fe's sister railroads.

With the right-of-way phase of Santa Fe's corrective surgery settled, that meant that the road, then, had (a) a big Diesel "in the works," (b) a new train program mapped out, and (c) the architecture of its raceway "on the boards" or under way. The basics were set. Santa Fe could, at that point, back-up and refine, and define, its programming.

By late 1934, finished plan-and-elevation drawings for its big Diesel hung on the wall of designer Dilworth's office at Electro-Motive—drawings that were done along chunky, no-nonsense lines, rather like Helen Hokinson's club-women in the *New Yorker* magazine.

Dilworth's design for that big Diesel called for two, *independently-coupled* body units (built by St. Louis Car Company), each to house a pair of 900-h.p. engines and, interestingly, introduce bizarre "eyebrow" cowls (air scoops) over the four ends of those units . . . burly bits of business by any standards!

Those Dilworth Diesels were scarcely what one would call "speed-lined" but, small matter; cosmetics would soon mask the

31

Richard Dilworth has often been called the father of Santa Fe's Diesel fleet. He was Electro-Motive's chief engineer at the time Nos. 1 and 1-A were built and designed Santa Fe's first streamlined Diesel units for the *Super Chief*. Dilworth secured his formal training in electrical engineering in the Navy. In 1910 he worked at General Electric building gas-electric cars. By 1913 he was assigned to experimental Diesel-engine development. On January 1, 1926, he started with Electro-Motive as chief engineer, and in 1934, under his direction, the first commercially successful Diesel-electric passenger locomotive was born.

Diesels' plain Jane configuration. Waiting in the wings was noted Chicago Industrial Designer Sterling McDonald, fresh from doing the interiors of the DC-3.

Already a practiced consultant to Santa Fe, McDonald's palette quickly sparkled with a whiz-bang paint scheme that was to detract all but the most jaundiced eyes from the workaday lines of Dilworth's Diesels and on to these colors:

a Cobalt Blue roof above a Scarlet stripe surmounted an Olive Green body based with a Tuscan Red stripe and deep Sarasota Blue undercarriage.

By God, folks would notice THAT engine! And, while he was about it, McDonald also designed a handsome sign and the distinctive *Super Chief* lettering on it, a sign for lighted display between the engineer's and fireman's front cab windows.

Again sub-totalling, Santa Fe, in further "midnight oil" sessions at 80 East Jackson, planned *The Super Chief,* eventual flag-bearer of the new fleet, to act as a downfield blocker for that fleet and serve also as a glossy showcase for the road's new passenger wares.

Obviously, *The Super Chief* that Santa Fe's "brass" had in mind was a sleek, stainless steel one—a racer—but, as John Morris said, "... it'll take 'em a year to build the damn thing! Why waste all that time? Hell, we got a whole damn pool o' cars over here for the *Chief . . .* why not pull out half a dozen and make-up a train to fill in while they're buildin' the damn streamliner?"

Motivated by Morris' backshop rhetoric and icy logic, it was, indeed, decided to release *The Super* in TWO stages: first, as a heavyweight, Standard Pullman stop-gap model with borrowed cars and, second, as an all-stainless steel train a year or so later.

Here, let it be said that, when Santa Fe did decide on a two-stage release for *The Super Chief,* right then and there, they rated high marks. Whereas other railroads had turned out their streamlined company-gems only as finished products, thereby losing precious train-exposure while their showpieces were abuilding, Santa Fe, on the other hand, would have a year-long "commercial" in its six-car, stop-gap, heavyweight *Super-1* and, once again, cagily steal a march on the competition.

At that point, Santa Fe needed its first road Diesel for practicing with and making shakedown runs—travels and testing so vital to a parent-newborn relationship.

2

I n August, 1935, Santa Fe finally took delivery of its newborn, bluntnosed power plants—numbered 1 and 1-A—and immediately dubbed them "Amos 'n' Andy," after the "rage" radio team of that time.

Done-up in the riotous finery that Sterling McDonald and Leland Knickerbocker created for them, sporting those big "eyebrows" over the ends of each unit, 1 and 1-A looked every inch the downfield blockers they were intended to be, and Santa Fe had them in-training in no time.

During the 9 months that followed, 1 and 1-A ran, walked and plodded the length and breadth of an engine-killing system—in all kinds of weather, as "light" engines or with full trains—and pulled everything but the foundation out from under the roundhouse. It wasn't long 'til Santa Fe knew that it had a pair of real comers in 1 and 1-A. No sir, not long at all!

1 and 1-A's businesslike execution of the obstacle-course that their new owners prepared for them set everyone to buzzing about the eye-popping sprints that the new Diesels had turned in, some at speeds of 117, 120, and even *150*-mph! Of course, "officially," Santa Fe said nothing about their new power's rip-roaring runs and, until today—forty-some years later—no mention has ever been made of those incredible 1935 speeds.

The original *Super Chief* locomotives Nos. 1 and 1-A ready for delivery in 1935. The truck shrouds were removed as they complicated maintenance. — WASHINGTON UNIVERSITY ARCHIVES

Luckily, men who did ride 1 and 1-A, daily, and lived those timings, are still around. What's more, *they kept notes!* One set of notes tells of a test-run late in 1935 when, roaring west, just out of Gallup doing "75," lead unit 1-A caught fire! Seems that overflow oil from the fuel tanks was discharged into the engine-room—oil broken into a fine spray by the blast of a ventilating-fan—and, in seconds, turned that room into a hell fire!

Burned men screamed and covered their faces as the locomotive ground to a screeching, grinding emergency stop—sliding three quarters of a mile—"flatting" 20 pairs of wheels on the eight cars behind. 1-A shuddered to an awful halt. Jumping into an ugly cloud of acrid smoke from raving hot brake-shoes, trainmen hit the ground, un-coupled the flaming front engine and, with "1," the second Diesel on that run, backed the train of cars away from the inferno to safety.

In a somewhat odd transference of duties, the Gallup Fire Department was called to the scene but, as the local paper put it, "lacked sufficient chemicals to put out the blaze." So, a steam

At the precipitous glazed face of Diesel No. 1 or 1-A was the piped, panelled, gauged and levered perch of the engineer who — with its throttle and brake valve handles — hurled-and-held the earliest *Super Chief.* — WASHINGTON UNIVERSITY ARCHIVES

1. Control and light switches
2. Forward and Reverse Control
3. Controller/Transition Lever
4. Throttle
5. Air Gauges: (L-R) Equalizing Reservoir; Brake Cylinder; Application Suppression
6. Windshield Wiper
7. Automatic Train Control Cab Signal
8. Automatic Train Control Acknowledge Switch
9. Train Brake
10. Locomotive Brake
11. Sander Valve
12. Bell Ringer Valve

Engine room of Santa Fe's Nos. 1 and 1-A. The passage way provided access to the 1,800 hp. motors. — WASHINGTON UNIVERSITY ARCHIVES

locomotive was set on an adjacent track and, almost quaintly, using the steam-discharge from a blow-off cock, shot out a stream of vapor and extinguished the fire.

Blackened and dripping water, 1-A was hauled, ignominiously, into Gallup, checked-over for four days, then sealed and, behind "1," dragged, lifeless, back to the Electro-Motive plant at La Grange, Illinois.

Five months later, after a rebuild, 1-A—with its also-modified twin, "1"—was out on the road and hard at it again, looking fit as ever. The Damon and Pythias Diesel-pair were destined for other hair-raisers . . . but more of that later on.

Nobody ever did find out just how fast 1 and 1-A would go. They knew they could take a train of six heavyweight cars—635 tons—from a dead stop to 60-m.p.h. in *under* two minutes! Seven cars took a little longer. And, if they left the throttle *wide open*, they could, and did, "rev" up to the just-mentioned 150-m.p.h. With a bit of restraint, say, with the throttle left in "Run 2" or "3" (to keep the Contactors closed), it was not hard to make 120-mph.

For the questioning, the watchful "eyes" of the cab's speed-recorders were averted from those careening romps at WAY over-the-speed-limit simply by stuffing a stick-match in the mechanisms.

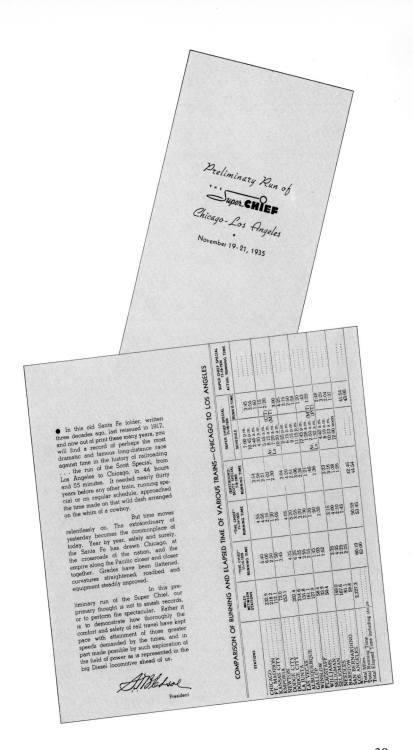

Preliminary Run of

THE

Super CHIEF

Chicago - Los Angeles

•

November 19-21, 1935

● In this old Santa Fe folder, written three decades ago, last reissued in 1917, and now out of print these many years, you will find a record of perhaps the most dramatic and famous long-distance race against time in the history of railroading . . . the run of the Scott Special, from Los Angeles to Chicago, in 44 hours and 55 minutes. It needed nearly thirty years before any other train, running special or on regular schedule, approached the time made on that wild dash arranged on the whim of a cowboy.

But time moves relentlessly on. The extraordinary of yesterday becomes the commonplace of today. Year by year, safely and surely, the Santa Fe has drawn Chicago, at the crossroads of the nation, and the empire along the Pacific closer and closer together. Grades have been flattened, curvatures straightened, roadbed and equipment steadily improved.

In this preliminary run of the Super Chief, our primary thought is not to smash records, or to perform the spectacular. Rather it is to demonstrate how thoroughly the comfort and safety of rail travel have kept pace with attainment of those greater speeds demanded by the times, and in part made possible by such exploration of the field of power as is represented in the big Diesel locomotive ahead of us.

President

COMPARISON OF RUNNING AND ELAPSED TIME OF VARIOUS TRAINS—CHICAGO TO LOS ANGELES

STATIONS	MILES BETWEEN STATIONS	"THE CHIEF" 11-14-1926 RUNNING TIME	"THE CHIEF" 11-14-1935 RUNNING TIME	(EASTBOUND) SCOTT SPECIAL 7-1905 RUNNING TIME	SUPER CHIEF SPECIAL 11-19-1935 SCHEDULE	SUPER CHIEF SPECIAL 11-19-1935 RUNNING TIME	SUPER CHIEF SPECIAL 11-19-1935 ACTUAL RUNNING TIME
CHICAGO					7:00 p.m.		
FT. MADISON	232.9	5.40	4.55	3.54	10:45 p.m.	3.45	
KANSAS CITY	218.2	6.00	4.58	3.21	2:40 a.m.	3.55	
EMPORIA	112.1	1.50	2.16	1.03	4:30 a.m.	3.50	
NEWTON	73.0	3.45	1.30	2.30	5:15 a.m. (CDT)	1.15	
DODGE CITY	153.1		3.05		Ar. 8:15 a.m. (MDT)	2.30	
LA JUNTA	202.4	4.35	4.05	3.04	Lv. 7:20 a.m. (MDT)	3.00	
LAS VEGAS	214.6	6.25	5.20	4.20	2:35 p.m.	3.25	
ALBUQUERQUE	131.8	3.55	3.55	4.51	6:15 p.m.	3.15	
GALLUP	161.1	3.50	3.30	3.06	9:15 p.m.	2.50	
WINSLOW	227.9	2.55	2.90	2.36	11:15 p.m.	1.58	
WILLIAMS		1.45	1.35	1.46	Ar. 2:28 a.m.	.20	
SELIGMAN	58.4	1.52	1.50	1.36	Lv. 12:45 a.m. (MDT)	.43	
NEEDLES	53.9				Ar. 2:50 a.m. (MDT)	1.20	
					Lv. 1:52 a.m. (PDT)		
BARSTOW	149.0	3.35	3.15	3.23	4:40 a.m.	2.48	
SAN BERNARDINO	167.6	4.35	4.00	3.16	8:19 a.m.	2.29	
LOS ANGELES	81.1	2.25	2.10	1.58	10:23 a.m.	2.04	41.54
	59.8		1.45	1.05	12:00 noon	1.37	43.00
Total Miles	2,227.3						
Total Running Time		60.10	50.59	42.46		41.54	
Total Elapsed Time including stops		63.00	53.45	44.54		43.00	

Doing better than "100," siren screaming, air-horn bellowing, Nos. 1 and 1-A explode onto a New Mexico crossing in a swirling cloud of red dust!

The one hairy-chested jaunt of 1 and 1-A that Santa Fe men—men *on* the engines—dearly loved to flaunt in the faces of their speed-boasting Eastern counterparts was the *regularly carded, all-uphill* climb of 3,466-feet from Chicago to La Junta—992 miles in 892 minutes—an *average* speed of 80.9-m.p.h! And with a heavyweight train of 7-cars—741-tons!

To be sure, running and sweating 1 and 1-A at such terrific speeds wasn't without penalties, sometimes severe ones. For example, once, on the string-straight stretch from Seligman to Winslow (east of Flagstaff), rolling at *120-m.p.h.*, they smashed to pieces the steel fans in the traction-motor armatures and, in the process, threw-off the armature banding wires at the coil slots and the commutator ends as well. The traction-motor roller bearings were completely burned out . . . the flying parts sounding like shells exploding.

Well, Santa Fe motive men wanted to find out if 1 and 1-A could take it and their engine-cabs were no places for faint hearts as they went about proving it.

Unlike any other Santa Fe locomotives, before or since, 1 and 1-A had on them, in addition to a pair of big Typhon air-horns, two electric sirens hidden up under the "eyebrow" cowls. Old engineers who ran 1 and 1-A on their test dashes delight in recalling how they used to roar down upon desolate New Mexico grade crossings, "widen on the sireen," and "scare hell outta Indians in buckboards or Model 'T' Fords."

For a moment, imagine, if you will, the hue and cry that those big Diesel brutes *could* raise—blasting across the red-earthed stillness of Navajo Land—with air-horn and siren both on, screaming and bellowing and spewing out their own pinkish cloud of dust along behind them for a half-mile!

It wasn't long, though, 'til 1 and 1-A's sirening ceased. It was short-lived because, all along the line, sleeping residents took an exceedingly dim view of the husky Diesels and, sometimes, nine heavy cars tearing through the hearts of their towns, often as not in the middle of the night, siren wailing like a banshee at every street-crossing. Accordingly, on the second trial-run out, 1 and 1-A's wild flights were, from then on, appreciably more sedate.

Sometimes, in those test-trains that 1 and 1-A hauled in the early days of 1936, there would appear a sparkling, flute-sided, stainless-steel day coach sandwiched among the old "heavyweights." That would have been No. 3070, the car that Santa Fe ordered from the Budd Company to be their first (for Budd *and* Santa Fe) standard-size, lightweight car. Delivered in January, 1936, "3070" was out and running, in the snow, in no time and, as a "tester" car, it and 1 and 1-A sort of grew up together . . . running in and with anything they were assigned to.

—Super CHIEF

It was an unseasonably warm afternoon, May 11th, 1936, when 1 and 1-A trundled into Chicago—tried-and-tested for almost nine months—washed up and settled back to catch their breath for the following day.

Over at Corwith Yard, swarmed on by busy work-gangs, sat four Pullmans, a Diner, and a Baggage-Lounge car,* poised and nearly ready to take their first *Super Chief* passengers to the Coast.

The car sextette glistened with fresh paint, their windows clean and shiny, and the brass railing on observation car *Crystal View* gleamed in the waning afternoon sun. Topping off that railing was a brand-new name-sign—a circle of Royal Purple—that Sterling McDonald had designed for *Super* service, quite possibly the best piece of logo-design any Santa Fe train would ever carry. The night came and all was quiet.

Morningtime at Corwith, May 12th, and they were stocking the six cars, still wet with the night's dampness—stocking them with provisions, wines, big cakes of ice, cut flowers, snowy bed linen, even the latest books and magazines—anything and everything that its well-to-do passengers might wish for.

Sitting on a parsley-laden baggage truck beside the Diner door, a knot of kitchen men washed and cleaned a box of fresh-caught whitefish, hosed-off heads of white-and-green butter lettuce, scoured bunches of fat asparagus and omnipresent potatoes, sorted through and cut off the stems of big, juicy Illinois strawberries, muscled aboard a crate of eggs and cans of milk and thick cream. There was lots to do.

By noon, Chef Henry Fauser and his white-hatted Fred Harvey crew were busy in the kitchen and pantry hanging short-loins of

---

*Baggage-Club No. 1301; *General Hancock*, 10 Sec-Lounge; Diner No. 1468; *Glen Frazer*, 6 Comp-3 DR; *Clover Knoll* 8 Sec-5DBR; *Cyrstal View*, 3 Comp-2 DR-Ob Lounge

Details of the coupling arrangement and multiple-unit electrical connection between units Nos. 1 and 1-A. — WASHINGTON UNIVERSITY ARCHIVES

Prime beef and pork, uncrating plump chickens, storing-away fragrant chunks of *Petit Gruyere* and English Cheshire in the coolers along with cloth-covered slabs of bacon, laying in tins of Malossol Caviar, and trimming pink cuts of veal.

The kitchen air was filled with the splashing of water and the clatter of pots and pans, air growing hotter by the minute from charcoal fires being laid in ovens, stoves, and broilers. Fauser and his staff bantered softly in thick, Mittel Europa accents as they went about their work . . . one sang, idly, verses of *Lieder.*

In the Pullmans, stocking-capped porters, their uniform coatsleeves bearing the service-stripes of many years—all of them well-up-in-years to even draw this *Super* run—also hummed esoteric melodies as they made up berth after berth with fresh linen that gave off that snuggle-down aroma that one could find *only* in a Pullman car.

Speaking of Pullmans, so often precious refuge for the author, the triangular-folded, blue-striped hand towel had a wonderful fragrance, the kind that made one hold it against the face a few seconds longer while patting dry just-lotioned or just-creamed skin. For that matter, nothing in all the world was quite like the variety of odors and sounds that, early of a morning, filled a men's washroom on a Pullman, *Super Chief* or otherwise, in the "good old days."

Herewith, a sampling of those odors and sounds: the snap-click of little lever faucets spurting water that, as soon as it hit the lavatory bowl, began to sway and slosh with the train's motion ... the clacking of wooden-handled shaving brushes whipping-up lather in milk-glass shaving mugs ... the mingled pungencies of after-shave lotions ranging from John Frederic's "Golden Arrow" down through "Eau Pinaud," "Aqua Velva," Bay-rum, and bottoming out with Witch Hazel ... the vigorous patting-on and rubbing-in of dryly flowery talcum sprinkled out of a brown-and-white striped can ... the ages-old counterpoint of hacking, snuffing, blowing, spitting, and, of course, farting ... the sudden-up/sudden-down roar of the wheels every time someone opened and closed the heavy, full-mirrored toilet door ... and, as a fitting close to the laving ritual, when one went out through the heavy cloth that curtained-off the washroom, the rancidity of freshly-lighted cigars went through that curtain too, and lingered in the nostrils. Ah yes, sweet remembering.

Back at Corwith Yard, it was getting on toward Four when a panel truck ground to a stop in the gravel alongside the observation-platform of *Crystal View*. The whistling driver opened the twin-windowed rear doors, dug inside, and began pulling out bunch-after-bunch of moist-petalled Gladioluses and Stock. He handed them up the steps to a workman on the platform who, in turn, handed them up to another on a stepladder, who then draped them across the end of the clerestory roof.

Between liftings, the man on the platform threaded "Glads" in and out of the brass railing 'til the entire platform—roof and railing—was bowered and buried under *color!* Thus arbored and brightened, they took the "blue flag" off *Crystal View* and sent it and *Super-1* on up to Dearborn Station behind a puffing yard engine ... well-stocked and all dolled-up to meet its public, for the first time, in about a half-hour.

The switcher gently nudged its polished six cars—last car first—into the grimy "throat" of old Dearborn and on back to where a length of red carpet ended behind ropes strung through 2x4s to form a makeshift railing at the bumper end of Track 5.

Braked to a gentle stop, Gladioli-bedecked *Crystal View* did look for all the world like the belle of the ball.

Sketch of flower-decked *Crystal Ridge* at Santa Fe's Corwith Yard, Chicago, as the author saw it on May 12, 1936.

Up ahead, the switcher backed off and, slipping over from an adjoining track, 1 and 1-A coupled on. The 12-cylinder Winton Diesels roared and spit sparks from a final "gunning" that Engineer Manley Marsh gave them. Duly warmed, they settled into a grumbling, rhythmic idle.

Marsh, 50-years-old, thirty of them with Santa Fe, set his brakes, shut off the bell-ringer, checked his gauges and, satisfied, backed his lanky, coveralled length out of the cab, down the ladder, and onto the platform where he and Conductor Tom Custer met, compared watches, and chatted briefly.

1 and 1-A were well known to Marsh . . . and vice versa. The quiet-spoken engineer who "ran as fast as the wheels would turn but was as safe as bread-dough" had romped the twin Diesels many times . . . so many, in fact, it was almost old hat.

Standing relaxed below the cab doorway, occasionally tugging at his long-visored cap, Marsh looked back along the six hundred and some odd feet of his train, somewhat bemused by all the hulabaloo going on at trackside. He smiled at chattering visitors shouting "goodbyes" to people on-board . . . passengers waving from vestibules . . . Western Union boys with last-minute telegrams ... red caps racing ... and, way at the very back, flash-bulbs popping and people cheering.

"That must be for the movie people," Marsh figured and checked his watch, which read "7:10:40." More distant flashes and Marsh stretched, beamed at a boy wanting *his* autograph, gave it and, with the grace of years of practice, swung his foot onto the first ladder step, pulled himself up the grab-irons and into the cab.

Fastening the chain that guarded the small door, Marsh eased himself into a cushioned seat and nodded greetings to Fireman Hugh Kelly and Diesel Maintainer Larry Brasher. "7:12:30" and others, mostly "brass," bustled about the narrow confines of the cramped cab, proof of the special status of *Super-1's* maiden revenue passenger run.

Marsh's practiced eyes roved from the train control panel with its cut-out lighted letters "H-M-L" to the glowing dials of train

Another of the author's hurried, on-the-spot sketches showing the first lash-up ever of the six-car heavyweight ***Super Chief-1***. Bloom-bedecked observation car *Crystal View,* leading the way — backing into Dearborn Station, May 12, 1936. At the right, the patch of red carpet behind 2x4's and clothesline for crowd control.

The Diesel-electric locomotive of Santa Fe's *Super Chief* as it got underway on its first regular trip to Los Angeles. (LEFT) Engineer Manley Marsh easing the throttle on No. 1.

brake, engine brake, and "Deadman" control gauges. His fingers touched and "placed" all levers and handles. Pulling a wad of "waste" out from behind an air line, he wiped the windshield, eyed threatening sky, and mused, "Might have some wet rail t'night."

"7:14:45" and a last look back, flashes really popping, then a big cheer. "Guess she's bustin' the champagne now," someone murmured. "7:15:00" and just above Marsh's head, Tom Custer's "Highball" tweeted harshly and, simultaneously, Kelly relayed the rear brakeman's lanterned "Go ahead."

Marsh twisted open the bell-ringer valve, flipped on the headlight switch, started the bell ringing, and doused the overhead cab lights. Darkness inside was punctuated by circles of red and green and the glow of dial lights. Easing the throttle open, Marsh velvetly gave 1 and 1-A their head. 3,600 "horses" snarled a path between two waiting steam engines and rolled heavily southward—on oily rail—into the yellowy-bright path laid by the headlamp.

Weaving in-and-out of clusters of freight and baggage cars, 1 and 1-A put their shoulders into the rails and rocked nudgingly to their lateral imperfections. The wheel sounds changed from clumps to clicks and the chain across the cab door swung in a wider arc. Marsh inched-back the throttle and the Diesels lunged ahead with watery smoothness.

The susurrant chatter of pistons and the drone of generators orchestrated the engine rooms as *Super-1* picked up speed. Beneath the steel floor, an harmonic vibration of power flowed and resounded. The stench of hot oil permeated everything.

Slapping over the Panhandle Crossing, thirty minutes out, they were into Lemont—twenty-five miles out of Chicago. In a few more minutes, Marsh slowed to negotiate crossings and crossovers at Joliet and, to no one in particular, said, "Can't make any time 'til we get away from here."

Beyond restraining Joliet, out along the Des Plaines, Marsh began to pour it on. Winding-up to "80," he was as busy as a xylophonist between whistle-cord and brake valve. Slamming into those Illinois Division curves at "85" or "90" called for a "perfect memory of the lines and a nicety of judgement born of long experience and complete concentration."

1 and 1-A, it should be mentioned here, particularly while we are aboard *Super-1's* first Diesels in 1936, rode so smoothly, so easily, that they beguiled even the most senior Santa Fe engineers who, often before they knew it, were going at far greater speeds than track or train could handle.

Marsh, however, uniquely surmounted the insidious subtleties of encroaching speed and, according to the men who rode with him in the cab, was so deft that "he could brake from 90 to 80-m.p.h. and back to 90 without detection, except, that is, for the sound of the train-line exhaust at the equalizing reservoir port . . . *after* it was over."

In "1's" cab again, the hiss of air was almost continuous for certain stretches. It began softly as Marsh approached a curve, rose to a sighing wail as he hit it fully, eased off, and then stopped as the track straightened and he throttled out to speed once again. Glancing aft, Marsh saw circlets of sparks at the wheels of the celebrity-filled Pullmans each time he applied the brakes. The red marker-lights on *Crystal View* trailed him smoothly and doggedly.

At the full impact of curves, Diesel "1's" headlight pointed directly out into the Illinois countryside. Then the unyielding rails stiffened and *Super-1* gave in to their dictum and, after a couple of grudging lunges, turned the arcs with a grace that belied its bulk and momentum. 1 and 1-A hugged the track tightly and the lighted rails, like a yellow grosgrain ribbon, flowed up dizzily and swept beneath the cab.

Trees and embankments blurred past the cab's side-windows and the sough of wind in the open cab door grew stronger. Perspiring, Marsh took a swig from a jug of iced water. At 8:45, *Super-1* reduced speed for a crossing and a cheering crowd at Streator; ninety miles in ninety minutes!

Cheers still echoing in their ears, 1 and 1-A took off, leapt ahead, and rocketed toward Chillicothe ... went up over Nine Mile Hill and hit 102-m.p.h. between Edelstein and Princeville. Grade crossings appeared with startling frequency and kept the air-horn steadily sounding its "two-longs, a short, and a long," the Diesels swooping down on stations where the curious kept back, pressed against depot walls.

1 and 1-A thundered on ... "90," "95," and better—bursting onto crossings, horn bellowing, "eyebrow" air-scoops setting up a turbulence that tore up dust, gravel, and debris and left a gritty wake of oil fumes and the reek of fiery brake-shoes.

Past Galesburg, Marsh slowed for crossing The Mississippi, slipped in and out of Fort Madison and, a mile-and-a-half down the road, braked *The Super's* six heavy cars to a rainy service stop at Shopton—*234 miles in 207 minutes,* almost a 90-m.p.h. average speed. Marsh had truly made his run with a flourish!

Easing out of his leather perch and, in the same motion, grabbing his valise, Marsh retreated from the humid cab and "slid" the grab irons down to a platform that was a hive of activity—porters, inspectors, car "tinkers," wagons of ice, flashlights, lanterns, hose-lines—everyone busy, no time to lose. A swarm of onlookers, up past their bedtimes for a glimpse of the new *Super,* added to the liveliness of the scene.

Turning, Marsh chirped, "Hello, Frank" to his "relief," 1 and

1-A's new engineer, wiry six-footer Frank Petska, who was slated to take the train on into Kansas City.

The Super was due out at 10:47 and, at "10:45:12," Petska "mounted to the cab" and took his place at the open side window. Petska, like Marsh, also had an eye for everything, a sort of concentrated nervousness which knew "all" and insisted it should be right.

Complications with a steam line kept the "blue flag" on and that nettled Petska. Droplets of rain gathered on the arm rest as the all-business engineer peered back and fidgeted. Five minutes late, "Highball" and 1 and 1-A drew away from the first-night crowd and accelerated past the shops and down toward the river. The inviting coziness of lighted Pullman windows flashed by. People were at-table in the Diner and, bringing up the rear, the clicketing wheels of *Crystal View*, whose flowered Lounge and railing swept off into the night . . . trailed by a plume of billowing steam vapor.

As *Super-1* plummeted into the blackness, rain spattered the windows of the Dining Car, a car alive with creamy light, snowy napery, jingling silverware, and clinking chunks of ice in heavy water-glasses—a snug enclosure of warmth casting aligned patches of its light out onto the embankmented right-of-way to chase the train in blurred pursuit.

Woodsy white smoke puffed sharply up and out of the charcoal broiler stack and bent immediately in the rushing wake of the train. The images of Chef Fauser's white-hatted crew flitted back and forth past the narrow kitchen windows . . . dashing from broiler to refrigerator to stoves to cutting-board and, finally, to the serving shelf . . . fashioning elegant meals and, all the while, fighting the gravity forces of their pitching, sweltering, narrow-aisled domain.

Though it was after eleven, first-night-out dinner was still being offered by stocky, graying, mustached steward Peter Tausch, already a legend in his time. The amiable, 51-year-old Austrian—guardian of Fred Harvey *haûte cuisine* for twenty-five years on the *California Limited* and *Chief*—sensed that this serving was truly a once-in-a-lifetime occasion and, therefore, he made no attempt whatsoever to diminish the dinner hour or hasten "last call."

The dining car menu the first night out offered many epicurean delights such as Grilled Lake Superior Whitefish, Chicken Croquettes, Lamb Chops, or Chef's Special Sirloin Steak with French Fried Onions.

The celebrities and "brass" thus lingered late over dinner, urged to gustatory excesses and inner delights by the melifluous accent of Tausch, who reasoned, "How often does someone have dinner on the first run of a train that'll go down in history?"

Tausch was eminently suited to guide and curry the tastes of the new *Super's* patrons, most, if not all, of them *habitués* of the *Chief* and, accordingly, accustomed to the engaging natural caterer . . . privy to many confidences and rewarded lavishly for his tacit ways.

On that rainy May 12th night, without menus, drawing only upon a mental "catalog" built over the years, Tausch moved about his diner with an easy assuasiveness—suggesting here, disdaining there—murmuring assent at a choice well made or lauding audibly a particularly appealing dish from the Fauser kitchen.

In amongst the theatre talk and business gossip, Tausch interspersed geographic sentence fragments such as . . . "New York sent us," . . . "fresh in from Duluth," . . . or . . . "we took on-board at Chicago"—all part and parcel of train dining as Tausch practiced it, dramatizing the far-trafficking aspect and providing abundantly and flawlessly for all who entered his diner.

Motion picture and radio star Edward G. Robinson was aboard the first westbound run of the *Super Chief.*

Stopping beside a solitary diner in a blue pin-stripe at a table for two, Tausch asked Edward G. Robinson about his most recent role in "Bullets or Ballots." The gentle, erudite screen "menace" answered between bites of a nicely charred pound of prime strip sirloin and sips of *Chateau Lafite '28.*

Down the aisle, Ida Cantor and two of her girls laughed and chattered, all the while doing justice to a succulent, done-to-a-turn, tantalizing brown platter of grilled whitefish. Papa Eddie Cantor, mere hours off-the-air from his last broadcast for Pebeco toothpaste, was in *The Super* barber shop indulging himself in what his daughter said was his favorite pastime on a train: "getting a haircut, hot-oil scalp rub, and a facial."

At mid-car, in a red suit and apricot blouse, Eleanor Powell, greatest of all the movie tap dancers, on her way to start "Broadway Melody of 1937," talked spiritedly and rhapsodized over a creamy parsley and chicken omelette flanked by the palest yellow asparagus in lemony Hollandaise. Rumor had it that the leggy Miss Powell spent a large part of that first *Super* trip—enough of it, anyway, to be seen by a goodly portion of the passengers—in "white silk pajamas" which supposedly excited or, at the very least, impressed her lissome figure on the impressionable. Today, "Ellie," still leggy, still dear, the lady who took opera-length hose to Olympian heights, doesn't recall the silken sleepwear but says, tongue in cheek, "Whatever I had on, it was better than being caught in the buff!" The new *Super* plunged on into the rain.

Unnoticed by his fellow diners was a thin, almost gaunt man in a gray sharkskin suit, lavender and gray-striped shirt, violet

53

Charvet tie, and a pink carnation *boutonniére.* The long-faced dandy, columnist O. O. McIntyre, on his yearly trip to California, stared moodily out the rain-splotched window but brightened visibly when a platter of sizzling, extra thin, panfried pork chops—bedded in a bower of watercress and parsley—was set before him. McIntyre, confessedly a meat 'n' potatoes man, aspirated accolades on his fork-cutable chops and seemed transported by the feathery Lyonnaise potatoes, beans *au beurre,* and celery Pascal.

Quite the other side of the coin, another fourth estater, New York *Daily News* sports writer Jimmy Powers and three thick-necked cronies roistered over a lemon-bordered, iced array of Malossol caviar—chopped egg white and chopped egg yolk *garni*—soon interrupted by the arrival of four helpings of cold prime ribs with beefsteak tomatoes and marinated artichoke hearts over which they wagered aloud who'd win the Olympic Games Trials in Philadelphia the following week.

Also absorbed in the Missouri rain splashing their window were Art Director Cedric Gibbons and his striking wife of not too long a time, Dolores Del Rio. Holding hands, the Gibbonses listened intently as Tausch recited dessert options and extolled the virtues of a particularly fine *1912 Port.*

Six-car *Super Chief-1* roaring westward on her maiden run near Las Animas, Colorado — moving so fast as to "bend" forward behind Otto Perry's focal-plane camera shutter the hazy morning of May 13, 1936.

Super Chief-1 at full cry — hurls her dirtied, greenish bulk through a Pasadena orange grove, dust flying, ground rumbling from her hundred-mile-an-hour onslaught as she nears Los Angeles on her maiden journey. — RALPH MELCHING

Taking in all the eating and menu ritualizing, smiling rather benignly and knowingly, was a recent arrival to the U.S., expatriated European designer, Hungarian-born Paul László, who well knew his way around fine fare, dining cars, and the good life. László, impeccably turned out in tweeds of a Stuttgart tailor, chose cosmopolitanly the prime strip sirloin overtured by caviar, followed by onion soup, asparagus Hollandaise, lettuce hearts, a blushing bowlful of strawberries and cream, and a *demitasse.*

James Montgomery Flagg, tall, craggy-faced, hawk-nosed . . . looking, in fact, very much like his famous "I Want You" poster, sipped cups full of black coffee and scrawled deliciously, inkily linear sketches on the back of a menu. Flagg was Hollywood-bound to do special art work on Frank Capra's "Lost Horizon." *Variety* explained that "Flagg's sketches will be used as key picture's for advertising campaign."

Just three miles from Santa Fe's La Grande Station of Los Angeles, the *Super Chief* is about to cross the Los Angeles River. A Diesel maintainer appears at the door of the cab after spending the entire run from Chicago to Los Angeles alongside 3,600 growling horsepower. — GERALD M. BEST

In all its glory, the first westbound run arrives at Pasadena with a throng of spectators on hand to view the new monarch of the rails.
— RALPH MELCHING

Ben Bernie, off to LA for a May 25th opening of his orchestra's engagement at The Ambassador's "Coconut Grove," Jean Hersholt, bound for 20th Century Fox to toss a luncheon celebrating his 30th year in films, and Carlton E. Morse, creator of the hit radio serial "One Man's Family," rounded out *Super-1's* late-late diners.

Sated with the *somptuosités* of Fauser cookery, the last of *Super-1's* dining car patrons bantered "G'nights" to Tausch, who rose—from stealing weary spoonings out of a cup of clam broth—to reciprocate. In the then-empty diner, Tausch slumped back into his chair, idly fingered the petals of a yellow rosebud and, for the first time that day, relaxed, took a deep breath, and stared out the window at the scudding rain.

A few of the hardier nabobs made their way forward, through a green-curtained aisle of Pullman sections, past drawing rooms, and on into the Club Car, the province of white-haired barman Albert Day, also a long-time fixture on *The Chief* and, like Tausch, a veteran confidant to the great and near-great riders of Santa Fe. Raucous conversations, swooshing siphon bottles, cocktail shaking, and the riffling of cards echoed about the lounge, either beckoning to join or signalling the less garrulous back to the quiet sanctuary and cool sheets of Pullman berths, sedately enticing with their dim blue night-lights.

By and large, the racing *Super-1* was calling it a day and no-where was the finality of it more apparent than in the observation lounge where a bowl of Talisman roses vibrated gently on a table beneath a low-lighted lamp, watched over by a lone brake-man—lantern at his feet—peering out the rear window. Only the sounds of the wheels disturbed his watchful reverie.

To paraphrase, in part, the closing line of the old movie trav-elogues . . . "and so we leave" the fast-moving first *Super Chief,* darkened windows, wet car sides, its rear marker lights diminish-ing like red tracer shells into the rainy night.

La Grande Station, western terminal of the *Super Chief,* looked more like a Hollywood movie set than a railroad station. This structure of Turkish and Moorish design, stood on Santa Fe Avenue between First and Second Street. (RIGHT) On the bright morning of May 14, 1936, first passenger Eleanor Powell is paternally hugged and rose-bouqueted by Engineer Galard Sloanaker, beside the looming, many-colored Diesel No. 1 of the titan-twins, Nos. 1 and 1-A. "Oh, what a beautiful morning," it was for the Train of the Stars.

During the fall of 1936, the *Super Chief* rolls into Pasadena under a blaze of lights. The station platform was always crowded with onlookers as they examined all parts of the unique twin locomotives during this time-exposure. — ERNEST M. LEO

Santa Fe's colorful ticket office in the Biltmore Hotel was busy with inquiries about the new *Super Chief.* — STAN REPP COLLECTION

On its second round trip, "locals" still lined the platforms of the beautiful Pasadena station to inspect the new *Super Chief.* One elderly railbuff, in the foreground, even brought along her nurse just in case the excitement was too much. — ALLAN YOUELL

One of the few action photographs of the *Super Chief* with the Nos. 1 and
1-A in regular service. In this scene, the eastbound *Super-1* scampers
through the mountain country of Northern Arizona at Winona, just 16
miles east of Flagstaff. — SANTA FE RAILWAY

Diesel locomotives Nos. 1 and 1-A were not always "star" performers. One of the units was having trouble between San Bernardino and Pasadena and No. 1333 was rushed to Pasadena to help bring in the *Super Chief* on time. (RIGHT) Coupling the No. 1333 to the ailing Diesel. —

BOTH PHILLIPS C. KAUKE

3

Three months before the heavyweight *Super-1* left Dearborn Station to ply its trade between Chicago and the Coast, work on Stage-2—the stainless steel model—was well under way in Chicago at the Merchandise Mart studios of 43-year-old designer-decorator Sterling McDonald, a name already mentioned.

It was well under way because McDonald had already spent two years designing in the lightweight-streamlined *genre* for Union Pacific's first two brown-and-yellow "bullet" trains—one that had set the cross-country speed record of 56 hours-55 minutes in October of 1934. Those trains were what attracted Santa Fe to McDonald in the first place; he knew his business.

Beyond his work for Union Pacific, McDonald had also put in a good deal of time designing the first lightweight day coach for Santa Fe—the one they numbered "3070" and took delivery of in January, 1936. From that design experience, McDonald had become rather facile with new trains and could, as Frank Lloyd Wright once put it, "shake them out of his sleeve."

McDonald's designs for No. 3070 plus the experience of working with the Budd Company engineers who, on that coach, ironed-out all kinds of structural and decorative features of full-size car building, uniquely equipped the Chicago designer to work on *Super-2*. He also found Santa Fe's wishes for *Super-2*—a train to be built entirely by Budd—easy to translate.

McDonald, first to start on *Super-2*, worked with the engineering and passenger departments at Santa Fe consulting on the interior design, color, and the coordination of it all. McDonald, you might say, was the "pre" in preliminary and he, along with Roger Birdseye, the railroad's advertising chief and resident expert on Southwestern America lore, set and developed the earliest thematics for the Indian motif that personified *Super Chief-2* and gave it such a remarkably distinctive continuity and coloration—perhaps the most distinctive ever to grace one train.

Even before he set to work at his studio, McDonald hied himself off to Santa Fe, New Mexico and the glorious surrounding countryside to soak up and sketch things indigenous to Indian land, such as the Bayeta serape-blanket which formed the design on the upholstery in *Navajo,* the bright-hued observation car. The colors in that serape—dug and picked from the earth—were exquisitely rich: earthy red background with blue-violet and cream patterns.

In his New Mexico journeyings, McDonald used up several sketchbooks—the cameo paper sheets overflowing with lithograph pencil and *Conté* crayon images. Out of the little pans in his Winsor-Newton paint box came gaily-colored pictures of Indian myths, legends, and ceremonials . . . many of them, up to then, forbidden to the white man's eyes.

At the risk of being textbookish, but in the interest of good "story," one such myth, the "Myth of the Mountain Chant," McDonald later painted on cork (to simulate sand) in charcoal and brilliant native colored-sands which copied the figures of four goddesses who depicted the "house made of dew-drops"— goddesses so tall they needed four separate skirts, one above the other. At any rate, McDonald's "Mountain Chant" sand paintings were the most arresting decorative elements in observation car *Navajo,* conversation pieces for as long as they were in that car.

To McDonald, the wellspring of Indian history seemed limitless, and it wasn't long 'til his portfolio burgeoned with studies, notes, and sheets of watercolored Whatman board—the exciting basic ingredients for the insides of *Super Chief-2*.

Stepping off the *Chief* at Dearborn on a chalky, bitter cold Saturday afternoon—February 15th, 1936—and weighted down by the spoils of nine days in the New Mexico desert, McDonald stuffed his bale of sketches and himself into a Parmelee cab and headed for the Merchandise Mart.

Settled, once again, in his cluttered studio, he spread his insouciant art work all over the floor and began culling through the *mélange*. With Roger Birdseye, by that time a regular visitor to The Mart studio, the innovative McDonald selected, rejected, reconsidered, set aside, squinted at and, finally, made his choice of what he'd use.

That very afternoon, he began to rough-out perspective studies of *Super-2* interiors ... picturing for Santa Fe just some of the many things that *could* be done, decoratively, in the cars of its first streamlined, *lightweight* train.

As the schematics unfolded, Santa Fe, a client warming to what it saw, urged on their designer to further study which—in the cases of the dining car and the observation lounge—resulted in the building of *full-size mock-up* sections of those cars in McDonald's studio-workshop.

Once Santa Fe officials could walk up to those mock-ups and stand, or sit down, right "inside" two of the four public cars proposed for *Super-2*, reservation, hesitancy, and/or opposition disappeared. So it was that a thoroughly briefed and genuinely enthusiastic staff of Santa Fe engineers left their Chicago offices on the afternoon of April 6th, 1936 and caught the *Broadway Limited* for Philadelphia ... well-prepared to talk train with the folks at the Budd Company, train builders *par excéllence*.

Budd and Santa Fe were not strangers to one another, having gotten acquainted originally, as the reader is now aware, in 1935 (the year before) when the railroad bought its first lightweight car—that stainless steel day coach "3070"—from the Quaker City firm.

As a matter of fact, Budd—with offices in Chicago in the same building and on the same floor as Santa Fe—had courted the railroad rather ardently ever since they, Budd, discovered early on just *how* far Santa Fe was headed into the realm of lightweight train operation and equipment ... a projected fleet of perhaps as many as 135-cars!

Even if the figuring was cursory, 135-cars could—if they built the *entire* fleet—net the go-getting Budds at the very least $9,-400,000, a sinewy, bell-ringing sum in those Depression Days ... and dollars well worth "going courting" over!

As it worked out, Budd, at the time busy as beavers and already at peak production with trains for other roads, still wound up with a great "consolation" order for 85 of the resolved total of 136-cars that would make up Santa Fe's lightweight fleet, earning a minimum of $5½ million for the Red Lion coffers!

For the record, Pullman-Standard, in Chicago, landed the contract for the other 51-cars of the Santa Fe fleet—plus six of the nine cars slated for a *Super Chief-3*—needed to make the Chicago-Los Angeles run a twice-a-week schedule.

Enough of exegetical prose; suppose we get back to *Super-2*, the reason why Santa Fe men were in Philadelphia and at the Budd plant on that gray, misty Tuesday morning, April 7th, 1936.

——Super Chief

In a tall, big-windowed room, gathered around a heavy oak table, were a dozen or more men scanning a mound of Sterling McDonald's drawings of train interiors. Some of his painted perspectives were stacked on a display easel at the end of the table. Cups of coffee rattled in saucers and thick cigar smoke, *de rigueur* atmosphere for conferences in those days, stained the air an odd blue. That meeting, viewed as a whole, was the first intercompanies idea session on *Super Chief-2* and all the rest of the cars that Budd was to build for Santa Fe.

McDonald had done his sketches and paintings expressly to provoke thought and to show the latitude that was possible in filling, decorating if you will, the tube-like cars . . . making them less tube-like. Precisely where windows, doors, and walls went would be for the Budd people and their own architects, Paul Philippe Cret, 50, and John Harbeson, 47, to settle once and for all.

McDonald's ideas were workable alright, but they were more thematic and decorative than nailed-down architecture. In any event, at that meeting the Budd men, particularly George Calhoun, looked and listened while the Santa Fe men explained, opined, urged, and as nearly every client does to an architect and/or builder, let it be known that they were in a fearful hurry to get the *Super* train going, literally and figuratively.

Calhoun and his compatriot at Budd, Walter Dean, the two men who would see *Super-2* through its birth pangs and structural development, asked countless questions in return, and as the morning wore on, came to realize that here—knowing better by the minute *what* Santa Fe wanted—would truly be a train unlike any that the Red Lion-Hunting Park people ever had made or ever would make. Both men suspected (and, as it turned out, history proved them right) that they were beginning a wholly unique string of seven passenger cars and, if the germinative features that Santa Fe already had on paper were any indication of what that train would turn out to be, possibly even a classic!

By the time the Santa Fe and Budd staffs broke for lunch, the conference table was a maelstrom of crumpled notes, scattered sketches and renderings, snuffed-out cigars and cigarette ashes— the litter so typically attendant to any confab.

Santa Fe specified these basics for *Super-2:* there were to be nine nonarticulated, standard-sized cars to sleep 104-passengers in "sophisticated surroundings" and house a crew of 12. For car buffs, the breakdown read: 32 in sections, 26 in bedrooms, 22 in compartments, 24 in drawing rooms, and a total "public" accommodation of 78 in the diner and lounges. Santa Fe required 1 RPO-mail storage, 1 mail-baggage, 5 sleepers, 1 diner, and 1 full lounge (with crew quarters and barber shop).

At lunch in the Art Alliance Club on South 18th Street, Budd's architects, Cret and Harbeson, joined the party and met, for the first time, the clients for whom they were to fashion *Super-2,* a train in which the design elements would fall together more artistically and elegantly than either architects or client could then foresee.

Several years ago, approaching ninety, Harbeson charmingly confessed to the writer that his all-time favorite train design was the one he did for the *Denver Zephyr.* Still, *Super Chief-2*—the train commission he was to talk about over lunch that dreary Tuesday in Philadelphia early in 1936—belied the eminent architect's pleasantly measured words of preference. The *Zephyr* was fine; *Super-2* was matchless.

Over cheese and fruit, sluiced warmly with brandy, Cret wrote vigorously on a note pad to Harbeson (in 1935, his larynx was removed), animatedly reviewed the comments and questions of the Santa Fe engineers, and particularly, expressed his pleasure at the refreshing car names that Roger Birdseye had selected for *Super-2.*

Taking his inspiration from pueblos and stations of the Indian country, the slender Birdseye chose *Isleta, Laguna, Acoma,*

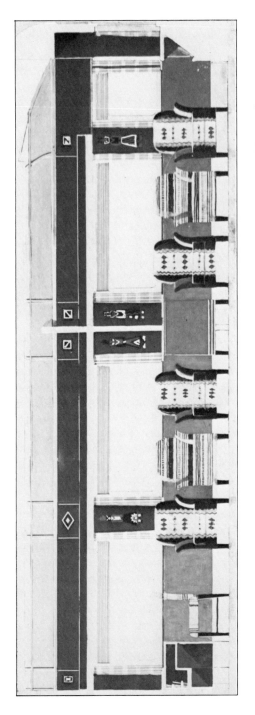

Once Santa Fe approved McDonald's schematic drawings of the train interiors, then Budd turned train architects Paul Philippe Cret and John Harbeson loose with the *Super Chief-2* project. This is a copy of the original tempera rough-study of the observation lounge in *Navajo* by Cret-Harbeson.

Cochiti, Oraibi, Taos, and capped them, most appropriately, with *Navajo,* the observation car. Those bits of aboriginal ancientry, Cret thought, were a good omen for the as-yet unborn train, and he smiled broadly as he downed the last sip of brandy and put on his raincoat.

In the six days that followed, Budd and Santa Fe went over the drawings, sketches, and whatever else McDonald had come up with again and again, worried about costs, asked about their train's documentable predecessors and, finally satisfied, signed the sales order for *Super-2* on April 14th, 1936.

With the essentials settled, Cret-Harbeson got the green light for *their* preliminary phase, *their* sketches, *their* drawings. So far as the car exteriors were concerned, patterns for primary structure and sheathing, the familiar ribbing on the roof, letterboards, skirting, and the fluting at the belt rails were already established in the Hunting Park plant's jigs and dies. To alter those patterns to any great degree would send costs skyrocketing; thus, outside, *Super-2* would be largely "stock" Budd.

Inside, however, *Super-2* was a horse of another color, and in spite of the fact that McDonald had made his preliminaries, filling car-shells "for keeps" meant still more research, study, and invention by the Cret-Harbeson office . . . and with precious little time to do it.

Both academicians, Cret and Harbeson, with a staff of ten in their Sansom Street office, approached the *Super-2* commission with thoroughness and an innovative touch. They commenced work on the final designs blessed with the same natural theme that McDonald and Birdseye had already discovered: the Southwest Indian country, dear to Santa Fe hearts and a font of legend, craftsmanship, and especially color, all of which Cret-Harbeson drew upon, too.

In six weeks, the Cret-Harbeson crew turned out their preliminary research notes, sketch studies, color perspectives (two schemes for each car), and along with fabric swatches and veneer samples, had them ready for Santa Fe's inspection and approval.

There were no such things as final working drawings (blueprints) on *Super-2.* The Cret-Harbeson *atelier,* as well as the McDonald studio, began their finish drawings, as we've said, at the end of May, 1936 and, as the train structuring went along, blueprints for that structuring were turned out to keep pace with the builders. As a matter of fact, some of draftsman "J." Morri-

73

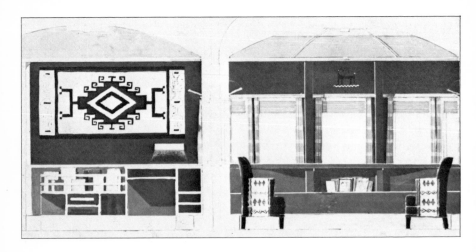

Additional Cret-Harbeson studies of the observation car *Navajo*. Their color perspectives and fabric swatches were approved and the project advanced to the "blueprint" stage.

From the office of train architects Paul Cret and John Harbeson came this charcoal sketch of Kachina panel back of the bar in lounge car *Acoma*.

Popular Mechanics carried this presentation rendering of *Super Chief-2* by its builder — the Budd Company. Although the art is somewhat impressionistic as far as the lightweight *Super-2* is concerned, it was placed upon a photograph whose locale is Southern California's famous Cajon Pass.

son's presentation drawings (numbered SK-12586) were dated as late as September 15th, 1936 . . . working drawings much later.

On Morrison's presentation drawings it says "designed and submitted" by Budd, pointing up graphically that even up to September, 1936, Santa Fe was still mulling over and deciding on *Super-2*. Considering, as time now permits us to do, that *Super-2* was delivered to Santa Fe in late April, 1937, the September, 1936 pondering by the railroad meant that there was just about six-and-a-half months left for building the train, a tight squeeze that obviated the need for those blueprints "as they went."

Here, another point does seem to bear mentioning. Actually, it demands exposing. *Super-2,* if it wasn't the most thoroughly planned train, must surely have been the second most thoroughly planned, designed, hovered over, carefully built single public train in an awfully long line of them.

Most new trains and, for that matter, remodeled ones were the products of a three-way creation process:

    1. The owner railroad decided how many passengers a train would carry, what sort of accommodations would be offered, and how much money was to be spent on a

AS THE SANTA FE GOES DOWN TO THE SEA

"Some day," said the Santa Fe's First Builder looking towards the setting sun, "our rails will go down to the sea . . ."

Along the Santa Fe Trail—one of the grandest marches in human history—the sand drifts in ruts that marked the passage of the wagon trains. Along the trail are great cities shining in the sun that scorched the eyes of the first adventurers. Indians talk in friendly commerce where war-shrieks seem still to echo. Explorers! Buffalo-hunters! Wagoners! Soldiers! Ranchers! And the Men Who Built the Railroad! There are the builders of the Santa Fe Trail!

But the great trek to the Coast is by no means ended. The trail has been broken. The West has been won. And the rails of the Santa Fe do indeed go down to the sea. But with the steady westward press of population a new need has risen. Time is now the measure ·of distance. Greater speed is necessary; but greater speed in safety and with all the comfort of modern civilization. And Budd has found the answer.

True to its great tradition, the Santa Fe carries the banner of this new achievement. With the inauguration of the great new Super Chief—a caravan of nine cars of stainless steel—the Santa Fe reaches the Coast as one of the leaders in the revolution transforming American railroads.

Budd trains of stainless steel now streak the West from the Great Lakes to the Coast, from the Twin Cities to the Gulf of Mexico.

Having proved by millions of miles of profitable distance run, that light-weight-with-increased-strength is the modern rule for railroad efficiency, Budd-built trains are giving new impetus, new life to passenger traffic. There is no form of transportation that combines more efficiently the factors of speed, safety and travel luxury.

Originator of ALL STEEL bodies for automobiles, now used almost universally, the Edw. G. Budd Manufacturing Company has pioneered modern methods in the design and fabrication of steel products.

EDW. G. BUDD MANUFACTURING COMPANY

PHILADELPHIA AND DETROIT

BUDD METHODS SAFELY ELIMINATE DEAD-WEIGHT

An advertisement of the Edward G. Budd Mfg. Company appearing in *The Saturday Evening Post, Collier's, Time, News Week,* and other national publications

The Edward G. Budd Manufacturing Company was so proud of its participation in the streamlined *Super Chief,* the firm placed this advertisement in *The Saturday Evening Post, Collier's, Time, Newsweek,*

A NEW Santa Fe Super Chief of stainless steel, with its striking interior design drawn from the picturesque Southwest and appointments the most modern creation of train builders, has taken its place as the newest "luxury" train of the West.

This new light-weight train, of nine cars and Diesel-electric locomotive, replaced the present Super Chief on the Chicago-Los Angeles run. It will maintain a schedule of 39 hours and 45 minutes for the 2,225 miles.

"The Land of the Navajos" provided the decorative inspiration for the new train. The cars were constructed by the Edward G. Budd Manufacturing Company of Philadelphia, and the locomotive was built by the Electro-Motive Corporation of Chicago.

The new Super Chief will faithfully represent the country and the people of the Southwest through which it flashes on its weekly run. Throughout, its decorative motif reproduces with fidelity the beauty of color found in the landscape, and in the Navajo's craft and ceremonial traditions.

Floor coverings, upholstery and color combinations used throughout the train have been matched with the colors so closely associated with the country. In addition, decorative designs have been selected to represent definite tradition. Photomurals depict the Navajo at work at the loom; faithfully executed wall murals show the ceremonial "sand paintings," all reproduced in natural sands of the desert, and lamps, wall hangings and shades show in each case the craft of the Southwestern Indians.

A remarkably harmonious note has been struck with the combination of the Navajo motif and the most modern use of color and design in the train.

Here a definite trend has been established in the design of a train as a fine residence for the traveler while en route. Each space has been designed minutely to give it the greatest comfort and convenience to the traveler, and colors and furnishings have been designed to make the journey restful. Cushions of soft rubber, built for the greatest ease, have been covered with soft yet rich materials. Walls are paneled in fine and rare woods and every fitting has been selected with both beauty and efficiency as the factors.

Even the cars take their names from the Southwest—Isleta, Laguna, Acoma, Cochita, Oraibi, Taos and Navajo.

The first two cars of the train include the post office, mail storage space and baggage compartments.

The third car, Isleta, includes sections, compartments and drawing room. The fourth car, Laguna, is similar in design.

The fifth car, Acoma, includes the cocktail lounge, bar, barber shop and quarters for the crew where they may rest even during the day runs.

The sixth car, Cochita, is the diner.

The seventh and eighth cars, the Oraibi and Taos, include bedrooms, compartments and drawing rooms.

The ninth car, Navajo, includes drawing rooms and compartments, with the rear section devoted to the observation lounge.

In each car, connecting doors allow the drawing rooms and compartments to be connected in suite arrangement.

The upholstery, shades, drapes, and curtains have been dyed and woven especially to satisfy the demands for color harmony and texture. The Navajo influence is apparent in the selection of fabrics, in the design of the curtains and the colors of the upholstery. The satin finished chrome plating on the hardware, which, although modern, is yet a silvery color.

The various woods and colors employed in sleeping rooms of the Super Chief are:

Wood	*Mouldings on Wood*	*Painted Surfaces*	*Floor Covering*
Avoidre	Flesh	Mist Blue Sulphur White	Carpet—Two Shades of Blue
Bubinga	Chocolate Brown	Light Sandstone Mist Blue	Linoleum, Sand with Black and White Border
Curly Maple and White Harewood	Aluminum	Perfect Blue Sulphur White	Linoleum, Sunshine Yellow and White
Figured Red Gum	Quarry Brown	Flesh	Carpet Mist Taupe
White Harewood	Light Cream	Lemon Cream Vienna Drab	Carpet Jade Green
Satinwood	Café au Lait	Blue Gray	Carpet Modern Blue
Macassar Ebony	Seal Brown	Peach, Light Chocolate	Carpet Rumba
Figured Aspen	Light Buff	Peach, Vienna Indian Red	Linoleum Brown Jaspe
California Redwood Burl	Light Chocolate	Light Cream Cocoa Brown	Linoleum Sable Jaspe
California Redwood Burl	Light Chocolate	Peach, Blue Gray	Carpet Mahogany
Figured Teak	Light Portland Brown	Colonial Yellow	Linoleum Sable Jaspe

The diner, cocktail lounge, and observation lounge cars very definitely show the influence of the art developed by the nomads of the great Southwest in their ceremonials.

In the dining room, the carpet has a reddish brown field with black insets and stripes; the side walls are veneered with Bubinga trimmed with chocolate brown mouldings; the end walls are painted sandstone brown, and the vaulted ceiling is flesh. Ebony finished walnut is used for the window sills, chairs, table legs and tops. A decorative buffet in ebony finished walnut is placed against the wall. This is surmounted by an overhead illuminated peach-colored mirror. The roller shades are faced on the outside with aluminum and on the inside with alternate stripes of white and pale yellow; and the drapes are of tan color.

Kitchen

The kitchen is no proud heir with a lineage extending into the far recesses of antiquity, but is instead the most modern of equipment. Its feature is the roomy, bright polished stainless steel interior. Included in the equipment are coal range, broiler, steam tables, steamer, coffee urn, sinks, dish washing machine, work shelves, refrigerators, ice cream cabinets, dish and silver storage spaces, and accommodation for carrying large food stores.

Cocktail Lounge

The cocktail lounge is trimmed with authentic reproductions of native Indian art set upon a background typical of the Indian country through which the train runs. The carpet is of desert sand color; the side walls are finished in Bird's-Eye Cypress with light brown mouldings; the upper walls and ceiling are finished with Primavera veneer with light buff mouldings; the window sills, desk, and magazine rack have ebony finished walnut tops. The vertical surfaces of the desk and rack are trimmed with Zebra wood to match the front face of the bar. The tables have black Formica tops with stripes of bright metal inserted in the edges; the large tables are mounted in wall sockets and have a hinged leg on the aisle side. The sofas and the small chairs at tables are upholstered with tan colored leather; the desk chair and the arm chairs are trimmed with henna colored fabric. In contrast with the brown tones which are so generously used are the satin finished aluminum bandings on the walls, the stainless steel structural mouldings and heater ducts, the horizontally black striped cream window drapes, and the true Navajo patterned roller shades with their black valance. Two items of particular interest are the inlaid wood back bar ornament and the rug hanging over the desk. The subjects displayed here are as a rule never executed in enduring mediums, as they are religious pictures, which in the past have been made of colored sand by the "Shaman" or medicine man on the floor of the living quarters. These "Sand paintings," as they are called, have lived between ceremonials only in the memory of the people, for enduring pictures are considered sacrilegious. The rug is true Navajo, and the back bar inlay is an authentic reproduction. Much credit is due Mr. Roger W. Birdseye, authority on Indian art, for the fidelity of the ornamentation.

Observation Lounge

The observation lounge in the last car also displays the work of the Southwestern Americans. In this room the setting comprises a desert sand colored carpet, copper colored lower side walls and a turquoise blue ceiling. The tables at the sides and end will be finished with dull black tops.

The desk and book case have Mexican parota tops finished in dull black, with bleached and weathered Mexican mahogany legs. The chairs and sofas are upholstered in true reproduction of native weaving, the original of which has been selected for museum display. The windows have brown drapes and tan roller shades.

The ornamentation of the pier panels employs authentic copies of sand paintings which occur in the story of Dsilyi 'Neyani, the "Myth of the Mountain Chant." These figures are executed in native colored sands and charcoal exactly as Navajo prophets have made them for generations. The four gods, North, East, West and South, of the second series of pictures are applied to the two end pier panels of each side. In the ceremonials, these were made on the sixth day, the white or east first, the blue or south second, the yellow or west next, and black or north last. The center piers have the four goddesses depicting the "House made of dewdrops," which comprise the third series of pictures. These goddesses are so tall they require four separate and distinct skirts (in the actual sand paintings executed on the floor of the lodge these figures were nearly nine feet high). The rainbow which would normally surround three sides of this painting has been transferred to the air duct soffit in the ceiling. The rainbow is adorned with tail plumes of the white eagle, the blue bird, the red flicker and the magpie. The fourth painting, showing the "Plumed Arrows," has been carried into the third dimension, but is otherwise true to size and color. Those arrows are the glow lights between the end windows.

A photomural of Navajo weavers at work on their looms, which hangs over the desk, and the rear table lamp with its ceremonial knife stem and goat's skin shade attest the decorator's fidelity to the motif.

Construction

Each of the car bodies is fabricated of 18-8 stainless steel by the exclusive Shotweld process into an integral unit. Fundamentally, the roof and understructure serve as compression and tension chords of a beam. They are connected by a truss, modified as necessary for doors and windows.

The doors throughout the train are so constructed as to fit flush and present a continuation of the body appearance when closed. Doors are of large size, and are split near the middle to permit opening the upper half without disturbing the lower half. They are fitted with folding steps, which, when not in use, are folded into the car body and present an appearance similar to the body proper.

Sleeper Design

The design of the sleeper sections has been developed so they offer more than usual privacy to the occupants, and more room. The upper berth tray is made flat on the bottom instead of curved, and moves from a nearly flat "day" position to its flat "night" position. Since the under side is flat, it affords more head room for the lower berth occupant. Two windows are provided for each upper berth. All windows are of shatterproof glass.

Air Conditioning

Conditioned air, composed of a controllable amount of fresh air from the outside and car air, is supplied to all passenger occupancy sections of this train. Both fresh and return air is filtered through washable metal filters before being passed over coils for cooling or heating. The subsequent delivery by insulated metal ducts furnishes air to all parts of the train occupied by passengers. Special branch ducts carry air to the berths of the sleeping sections.

The equipment is operated on the steam ejector principle, with the refrigerating equipment mounted below the car floor, and cooling equipment mounted between the false ceiling and the roof. The temperatures are controlled by thermostats.

Water System

All service water for the passenger cars is carried in stainless steel tanks mounted under the cars, from which it is delivered by air pressure to the various outlets. The system used in the dining car is similar, except for the addition of overhead storage tanks, one for hot water and one for cold filtered water.

and other national publications. Very few carried the *second* page which gave many details of the train consist and the many advancements in railroad carbuilding.

train . . . the latter, it hardly need be said, had the far-
thest reaching and, sometimes, most detrimental effect
on what a budding train would look like;

2. The industrial designer and/or architect was brought
in to interpret the wants and needs of the railroad and,
accordingly, to prepare the faces and furnishings that
a train would show to the public or its riders;

3. The builder, primarily structurally oriented, saw to it
that the car-shells, car-linings, partitions, sleeping
berths, air conditioning, heating, lighting, etc. were
feasible and buildably sound.

Super-2, however, went them all two steps better: it had *five*
progenitors of its physical makeup: the usual three plus an extra
designer-decorator (Sterling McDonald) and a second architect
(John Harbeson). So, Santa Fe said what *ought* to be done;
McDonald showed what *could* be done; Budd told what *had* to be
done; Cret-Harbeson drew up what *was* to be done.

—Super CHIEF

For all its color and striking detail, what really made *Super-2*
(the first lightweight *Super*) and set it far above any train Santa
Fe had ever made or ever would make, was a material specified
by John Harbeson. The material was *Flexwood Veneer,* and he
used it with consummate facility.

In *Flexwood*—nothing more than a thin (1/85 of an inch) layer
of wood mounted on canvas—Harbeson found an open-sesame to
design effects of the broadest range, and with it gave *Super-2* a
warmth and presence that made even oldtimers in the business
marvel.

Equipped with this palette of woods from the deepest to the
brightest shades, Harbeson "painted" interiors of such refined elegance that they are unmatched to this day. Varying the treatment in each car of the train, Harbeson made *Super-2's* seven
passenger cars a self-contained design unit and he did it in such a
way that the transition from car to car was experienced rather
than noticed. A Santa Fe "ad" man hit the nail on the head when
he wrote "the Super Chief is beauty wrought in wood."

The *Flexwood* names in themselves made for pretty heady
reading and a Santa Fe booklet, "Exquisite Interiors," lists those
names in a few neatly turned phrases:

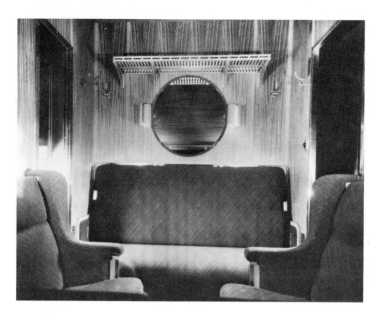

The vibrant goldness of Satinwood above powder blue upholstery and deep blue carpeting made for an exquisite interior in the *Navajo* Drawing Room. — SANTA FE RAILWAY

"Bubinga, White Harewood, Macassar Ebony, Avodire, Ribbon Prima Vera, Zingana—on and on runs the catalogue of rare and beautiful woods, drawn from the four quarters of the globe, that have been applied, in Flexwood Veneers, in the finish of the cars of the new streamlined *Super Chief.* Brazilian Rosewood, Ebonized Maple, American Holly, Redwood Burl, Gumwood, Teak, Aspen, and Satinwood—from the jungles of Burma and West Africa and the Ivory Coast they come, from North America, South America, and Europe. And behind each there is that rich story of man's everlasting search for beauty, regardless of time and distance and circumstance."

Keeping technical talk and decorative esotericizing to a bare minimum, by late summer 1936 the McDonald and Cret-Harbeson offices and the Budd plant had set a steady pace with the streamlined *Super Chief-2,* and out of their day-by-day drawings, delineations, and calculations, cars grew and flourished. Rough-surfaced underframes soon sprouted walls, and it wasn't long 'til the monotonous snap of the "Shotwelder" took over.

"Shotwelding" was Budd's bread-and-butter item which, in a

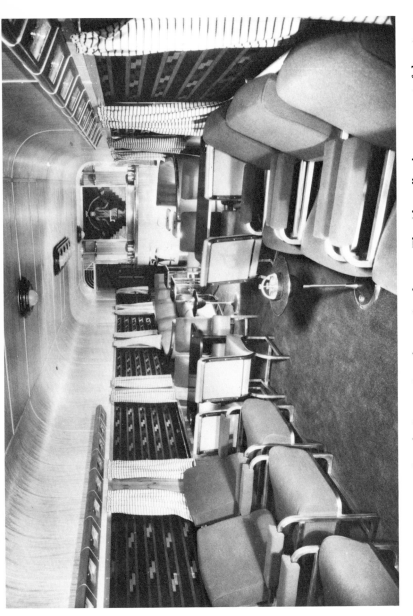

Lounge car *Acoma* gives the impression of exceptional space. The side walls, above a carpet of desert sand coloring, were finished in Bird's-eye Cypress, while the upper walls and ceiling were a light tan prima vera. — SANTA FE RAILWAY

few words, worked like this:

> *Two pieces of stainless steel are welded together by means of the passage of a measured 'shot' of electricity— strong enough to melt together touching surfaces, but of such short duration that the exterior surfaces are not altered.*

Ordinary spot welding, by the way, alters the composition of the alloy *at the surface* so that it is no longer "stainless." What's more, it changes color and rusts. So much for the welding of stainless steel, *Super-2's* cloak material.

As they will in any building venture, problems unsettled the *Super-2* program from time to time. For one thing, getting the *Flexwood* to adhere to the masonite backing-panels was, according to Harbeson, a difficult matter to solve. Then, too, manufacture of the Indian-motif fabrics for the observation-lounge chairs, laid out with great care by McDonald and Darwin Urffer, wasn't at all as it should have been. Although "woven" patterns were specified, cost-consciousness reared its ancient head and some of the upholstery material arrived at Hunting Park *printed* with dyes!

To illustrate, for just a moment, *how* carefully the fabric designs for *Super-2* were first planned, the weaving mill was instructed to arrange its Jacquard cards to drop a stitch now and then to simulate the handwoven look. Think of it: handwoven fabric on a public train!

Other points, more worrisome than difficult, needed looking after: noise, vibration, corrosion, air filtration (near-half of *The Super's* route was harsh-sanded desert), and the wearing-qualities of materials. But liberal amounts of study at the old drawing boards cancelled out those irritants and *Super-2* continued to develop, right on schedule, growing handsomer by the day.

In the Budd sign shop, at a paint-spattered easel using a home-made Mahl-stick, Tom Claiborne was hand-lettering one of the stainless nameplates, glancing occasionally at a scaled layout blueprint from the Cret-Harbeson office. Nameplates under way, it wasn't long until the car-shells had shed their metallic anonymity and been dignified with specific identities: *Isleta, Laguna, Acoma, Cochiti, Oraibi, Taos,* and *Navajo* was how they would be known from then on.

Leland A. Knickerbocker, book-illustrator turned train-illustrator, produced this stylish rendering of *Super Chief-2*'s new Diesel locomotive for General Motor's Industrial Design Department. Santa Fe's No. 2, the first red-nose Diesel, was to replace hard-working Nos. 1 and 1-A (known as "Amos 'n' Andy" by operating personnel). Note the obvious triumph of the Diesel over steam power. — M. E. ICZKOWSKI COLLECTION

4

W hile *Super-2's* seven passenger cars took shape in Philadelphia, Electro-Motive, at La Grange, Illinois, was breathing life into a new Diesel locomotive to replace hard-working 1 and 1-A, old "Amos 'n' Andy," after their arduous, engine-bursting stint testing and hauling *Super-1*, the heavyweight "downfield blocker."

Behind a door marked "Streamline Train Department," in a long, north-lighted, slightly cluttered studio room, shirt-sleeved and wearing a green celluloid eye shade, artist Leland A. Knickerbocker, 43, hunched over a large drawing table. Knickerbocker, book-illustrator turned train-illustrator, had before him the rakish perspective of what could well have been an elongated automobile.

Dipping a No. 7 brush into a puddle of crimson poster paint at the edge of his butcher-pan palette, Knickerbocker rendered the nose of that automobile-like shape, actually the hood of *Super-2's* own Diesel. The crimson hood had replaced the air-scoop cowls or "eyebrows" of 1 and 1-A and a narrow band of that red color ran the length of both units at floor height suggesting, as Knickerbocker said, "the profile of an Indian head and the trailing feathers of a war bonnet."

Across the brilliant red nose (hood, if you prefer it) Knicker-bocker emblazoned a bright yellow *elliptical* Santa Fe herald ... the circular one had thus given way to industrial design modification. But, heraldic revision or not, *Super-2's* crimson nose with its yellow insignia went on to become, and to remain, as familiar a symbol as the boulevard-stop sign.

A companion facet of the fame of Santa Fe's first red-nosed Diesel was Knickerbocker's February 17th, 1937, once-in-a-blue-moon illustration of it: a painting that became so identifiable ———on-sight recognizable———with *Super-2* that Santa Fe, even after the train was built and photographed, continued to use the dazzling-colored Knickerbocker illustration in its various advertising and publicity releases.

Happily, what was for over forty years thought to be an anonymous piece of artwork becomes, with this book, identifiable at last as Leland Knickerbocker's best known work of a life that ended just three years later.

Super-2's new red-nosed Diesel was a two-unit, 3,600-h.p. model like 1 and 1-A, but there the similarity ceased. Looking at the eighth-scale clay model of it, sitting on a dais in the middle of the EMC studio, one could see at a glance that this pair had vastly better lines———sheathed in stainless steel———and *looked* like goers.

Above and slightly behind the new Diesel's automobile-like hood was the equally automobile-like windshield of a cab so spick-and-span that it brought about a complete change of dress among the sharp-eyed men who occupied it. Overalls were out and business suits or sport shirts blossomed on engineers and firemen alike.

Beyond and below the insulated back wall of that cab, all sorts of things had been added, or existing ones improved, since 1 and 1-A had left La Grange. AREA E-11-X axles, trunkline alarm systems, Satco-lined bearings, 12-point exhaust pyrometers, and Gardner-Denver compressors were there and waiting to quicken the pulse of any 1936 mechanophile.

Summed up, the second *Super-Chief* Diesel combine was a "beaut." For a stickerprice of $279,619.02, Santa Fe had gotten more than its money's worth!

5

At dawn on April 27th, 1937, had you stood in the yard of the Budd Company's Hunting Park plant in Philadelphia, an unforgettable sight could have been your reward for braving the chill hour. There, on a set-out track covered with a fine layer of night frost, was the glistening end product of exactly one year's thought and labor ... the completed *Super Chief-2*. It had been finished the night before and then rolled outside to spend the dark hours in inanimate solitude, contemplating a future many miles from this corner of "Philly's" Nicetown section.

As the sun rose higher, *Super-2's* 716-foot length of gleaming stainless steel was reflected crisply in scattered puddles and grease slicks indigenous to any and all places where rails and machinery mingle. Out of that striking string of nine cars, six would live to celebrate a Silver Anniversary. But that April mid-morning was a beginning, a glory day for *Super-2*, and hardly the time for sober talk of life expectancy.

The remainder of April 27th was given over to Richard Dooner for photographing the train, inside and out (mostly inside), touching up here and there, and just admiring *Super-2*. Perhaps, the writer has long felt, Budd men knew instinctively that they

Observation car view of *Super Chief's* Budd-built *Navajo* taken at Corwith Yard in Chicago during May of 1937. The purple drumhead sign was illuminated at night. — SANTA FE RAILWAY

would never see her likes again. Time has proven them right: there *was* only one *Super-2*, ever, from many standpoints.

On April 28th, *Super-2* took a leg-stretching trial spin over a Philadelphia belt line to loosen its structural stiffness, got a squirt or two of aluminum paint on dirtied journal boxes, and then went back again to the set-out track to await the following morning.

Around eight or nine o'clock on April 29th, a murky and drizzly morning, without ribbon-cutting or ceremony of any kind, *Super-2* took leave of its Hunting Park birthplace. Later that afternoon, tucked in among the maroon cars of the Pennsylvania Railroad's *Commercial Express*, sticking out like nine shining silver knives, *Super-2*——ignominiously sandwiched between dusty baggage and mail cars——was on its way for next-day delivery to its expectant owners in Chicago.

Sure enough, right on time, she was there the next morning and, after a bit of switching, shunting, and turning, a Santa Fe yard engine, puffing proudly and blowing its whistle boisterously and often, backed the sparkling-new *Super-2* into Corwith Yard where, hokey as it may sound nowadays, to the cheers of the yard gang, she came to a silken stop . . . home at last!

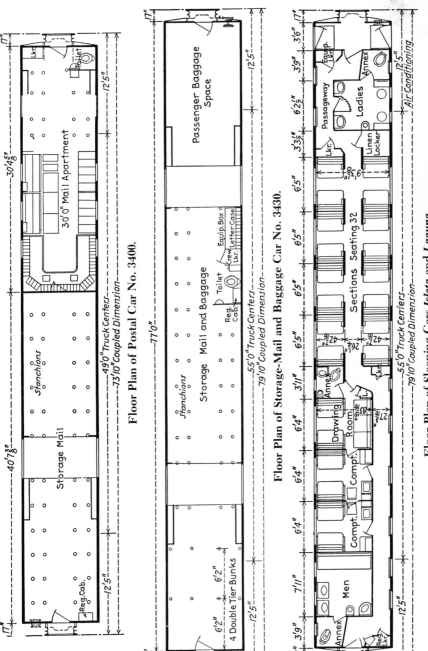

Floor Plan of Postal Car No. 3400.

30'0" Mail Apartment

Storage Mail

Stanchions

Lkr.

Toilet

Reg. Cab.

12'5"

30'4⅝"

40'7⅜"

1'7"

49'0" Truck Centers

73'10" Coupled Dimension

12'5"

Floor Plan of Storage-Mail and Baggage Car No. 3430.

Passenger Baggage Space

Storage Mail and Baggage

Stanchions

Toilet

Equip. Box

Letter Case

Crew

Lkr.

Reg. Cab.

4 Double Tier Bunks

6'2" 6'2"

7'7"

12'5"

1'7"

17"

12'5"

55'0" Truck Centers

79'10" Coupled Dimension

12'5"

Floor Plan of Sleeping Cars *Isleta* and *Laguna*.

Equip. Lkr.

Annex

Ladies

Passageway

Linen Locker

Lkr.

Sections   Seating 32

Drawing Room

Annex

Compt.

Compt.

Men

Annex

Reg. Lkr.

9'3⅞"

3'6"

3'9"

6'2½"

3'3½"

6'5"

6'5"

6'5"

6'5"

42⅛"

26¼"

42⅛"

3'11"

6'4"

6'4"

6'4"

7'11"

3'9"

1'7"

18'3½"

2'1"

12'5"

12'5"

2'5"

Air Conditioning

55'0" Truck Centers

79'10" Coupled Dimension

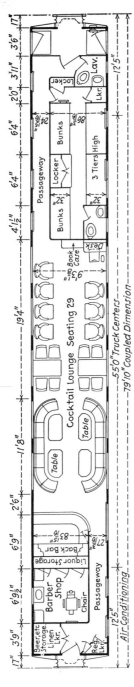

Floor Plan of Lounge Car Acoma.

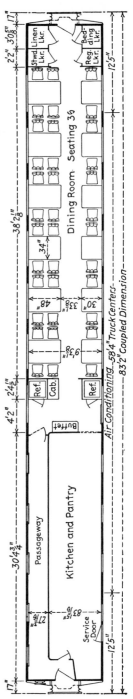

Floor Plan of Dining Car Cochiti.

88

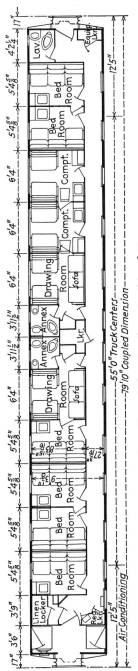

Floor Plan of Sleeping Cars *Oraibi* and *Taos*.

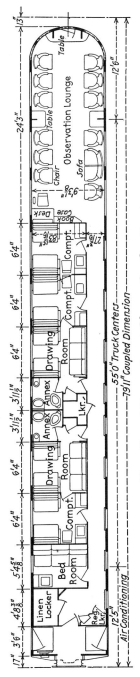

Floor Plan of Compartment-Observation Car *Navajo*.

6

For two weeks (May 3–17, 1937), *Super-2* did what most new trains were required to do: exhibited itself, submitted to interminable trackside eulogizing, ran *gratis* windsprints system-wide, loaded down with "industrial and civic leaders" and the press (most of whom would forget to talk about or write about their free *Super* rides) . . . and did it all with boundless mechanical agreeability.

The initial *Super-2* special run (Santa Fe looked askance at the word "publicity") was to be the first of *four* and, beside unveiling the cars, the Electro-Motive crimson-nosed Diesel, No. 2, was also slated to make its bow to the public at the head end of Santa Fe's new Flag Bearer. However, No. 2 wasn't quite ready at La Grange so, to the immeasurable delight of train purists, "regular steam locomotives," as the June, 1937 *Santa Fe Magazine* explained, "were pressed into service."

About that first "Special Trip," a four-day jaunt from Chicago to Santa Fe, New Mexico and back, Santa Fe's house organ had this to say:

> While this was not expected in any way to be an accelerated run, steam locomotives alone were used, the train often registered more than 90 miles an hour enroute———and no one was aware of any burst of speed.

During the first two weeks of May, 1937, *Super Chief-2* exhibited itself along the mainline between Chicago and Los Angeles. In this scene, *Navajo* cants to a curve and speeds off toward Lamy, New Mexico, on May 6, 1937.

Joseph E. Chapman, Pullman service veteran of 39 years, at the door to *Navajo* the night of May 8, 1937, just before the **Super Chief-2's** second "preview" run — Chicago to Los Angeles. Chapman was a favorite of Hollywood and Broadway stars.

Ignoring Santa Fe's thinly veiled though understandable deprecation of their prowess, the steam locomotives that were used, no doubt sensing the import of the situation, rose to the occasion and took the *Super-2* preview special skimming on its way to old Santa Fe, asserting with a vengeance their soon-to-be-usurped speed-making capabilities. Unfortunately, the steamers' display of power, though gallant and well-attended, was to no avail.

Besides offering the Fourth Estaters and various echelons of notability the speed and luxuriousness of *Super-2*, Santa Fe and Fred Harvey saw to it that their guests' personal wants ... anything from newspapers to cigars to pajamas to bouquets for the ladies ... were amply taken care of. Fred Wendell and Peter Tausch of Fred Harvey provided bountifully and lavishly for the culinary and libatory appetites of the peripatetic executives and editorializers and a glance at the gray card, price-free menus for the trek to Santa Fe tells graphically how well they fared at-table.

At the left, with his silver salver weighty with still-sizzling Filet Mignon *Jardiniere,* waiter "Wixie" Wilson serves Edward G. Budd, president of the Budd Company (left), and table companions their preview-run dinners. (LOWER LEFT) Between Las Vegas and Santa Fe, New Mexico, Maida Lopez and Olinda Rodriguez, with their Mariachi musicians entertain "preview" riders finishing their morning breakfast. (BELOW) Steward Peter Tausch offers Roger Birdseye, the Santa Fe's advertising chief, an after-lunch Santa Fe cigar during a *Super-2* "preview" run.

The wide-angle lens gave *Navajo* a long and graceful appearance when she posed for Indian admirers at Santa Fe, New Mexico, on May 5, 1937.

Industrial designer Sterling McDonald points out one of his design features to creative cohort Roger Birdseye (right), chief of Santa Fe's Advertising Department.

Edward G. Budd (left), president and chairman of the Budd Company, builder of *Super Chief-2,* chats with Lee Lyles (right), Santa Fe's director of Public Relations at the proscenium end of lovely *Navajo* on the "preview" trip to Santa Fe, New Mexico, on May 3, 1937.

The photographer on the "preview" run to Santa Fe took this photo-art piece for President Samuel T. Bledsoe of the Santa Fe Railway. A print was made during the layover and mounted on a 16x20 piece of art board. All passengers aboard that day signed the mount, including all members of the train crew.

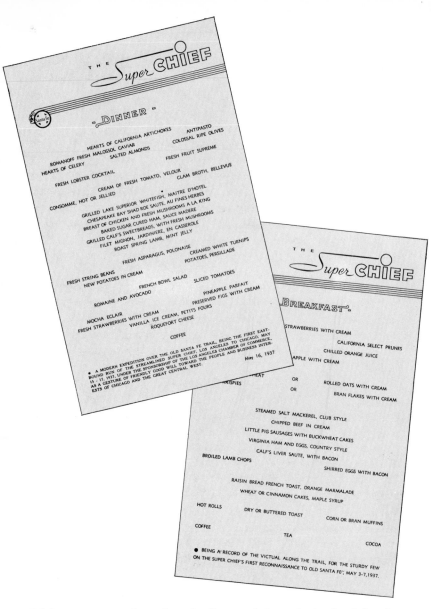

THE Super CHIEF

DINNER

HEARTS OF CALIFORNIA ARTICHOKES
ANTIPASTO
ROMANOFF FRESH MALOSSOL CAVIAR
COLOSSAL RIPE OLIVES
HEARTS OF CELERY   SALTED ALMONDS
FRESH FRUIT SUPREME
FRESH LOBSTER COCKTAIL

CREAM OF FRESH TOMATO, VELOUR
CLAM BROTH, BELLEVUE
CONSOMME, HOT OR JELLIED

GRILLED LAKE SUPERIOR WHITEFISH, MAITRE D'HOTEL
CHESAPEAKE BAY SHAD ROE SAUTE, AU FINES HERBES
BREAST OF CHICKEN AND FRESH MUSHROOMS A LA KING
BAKED SUGAR CURED HAM, SAUCE MADERE
GRILLED CALF'S SWEETBREADS, WITH FRESH MUSHROOMS
FILET MIGNON, JARDINIERE, EN CASSEROLE
ROAST SPRING LAMB, MINT JELLY

FRESH ASPARAGUS, POLONAISE
CREAMED WHITE TURNIPS
POTATOES, PERSILLADE
FRESH STRING BEANS
NEW POTATOES IN CREAM
FRENCH BOWL SALAD   SLICED TOMATOES
ROMAINE AND AVOCADO
PINEAPPLE PARFAIT
PRESERVED FIGS WITH CREAM
MOCHA ECLAIR
FRESH STRAWBERRIES WITH CREAM
VANILLA ICE CREAM, PETITS FOURS
ROQUEFORT CHEESE

COFFEE

● A MODERN EXPEDITION OVER THE OLD SANTA FE TRAIL, BEING THE FIRST EAST-
BOUND RUN OF THE STREAMLINED SUPER CHIEF, LOS ANGELES TO CHICAGO, MAY
15 - 17, 1937, UNDER THE SPONSORSHIP OF THE LOS ANGELES CHAMBER OF COMMERCE,
AS A GESTURE OF FRIENDLY GOOD WILL TOWARD THE PEOPLE AND BUSINESS INTER-
ESTS OF CHICAGO AND THE GREAT CENTRAL WEST.
May 16, 1937

THE Super CHIEF

BREAKFAST

STRAWBERRIES WITH CREAM
CALIFORNIA SELECT PRUNES
CHILLED ORANGE JUICE
APPLE WITH CREAM

...KRISPIES   ...EAT   OR   ROLLED OATS WITH CREAM
OR   BRAN FLAKES WITH CREAM

STEAMED SALT MACKEREL, CLUB STYLE
CHIPPED BEEF IN CREAM
LITTLE PIG SAUSAGES WITH BUCKWHEAT CAKES
VIRGINIA HAM AND EGGS, COUNTRY STYLE
CALF'S LIVER SAUTE, WITH BACON
BROILED LAMB CHOPS
SHIRRED EGGS WITH BACON

RAISIN BREAD FRENCH TOAST, ORANGE MARMALADE
WHEAT OR CINNAMON CAKES, MAPLE SYRUP
HOT ROLLS   DRY OR BUTTERED TOAST
CORN OR BRAN MUFFINS
COFFEE   TEA   COCOA

● BEING A RECORD OF THE VICTUAL ALONG THE TRAIL, FOR THE STURDY FEW
ON THE SUPER CHIEF'S FIRST RECONNAISSANCE TO OLD SANTA FE', MAY 3-7, 1937.

Dining car menus from "preview" runs of *Super-2*. At the right, the breakfast menu from the "reconnaissance" to old Santa Fe, New Mexico, between May 3-7, 1937. (LEFT) Dinner menu from a Los Angeles to Chicago "preview" under the sponsorship of the Los Angeles Chamber of Commerce between May 15-17, 1937.

Tuesday and Wednesday, May 4th and 5th, 1937, while *Super-2's* guest riders————in automobiles supplied by Santa Fe————roamed the Teseque Valley or lazed at the La Fonda Inn, a Lucullan buffet was spread in diner *Cochiti* for New Mexican politicos and "press" . . . again, catering of dubious, if any, dividend.

Late in the day, Santa Fe's citizenry, liberally sprinkled with cowpokes, Indians, and school children whose prospects of ever riding it were as remote as snow in the Sahara, were "permitted to pass through" *Super-2* and, at the sight of such confluent sophistication, shuffled wonderingly along the canvas runners laid over the richly carpeted aisles and corridors. The locals got a good look at the "wonders" of an on-going succession of exotically wood-lined berths, staterooms, and public rooms, made all the more inviting and beckoning by the ropes that kept them tantalizingly out of their reach and touch.

Thursday morning, May 6th, its complement of seventy-two "complimentaries" well wined-and-dined . . . all but inured to the seven passenger cars that they were, after all, brought along to see and report on, *Super-2* steamed (yes, steamed) out of Santa Fe, headed down to Las Vegas, turned left, and hurried back to Chicago.

Reviewing the four days in New Mexico, *Santa Fe Magazine* synopsized . . . "All was serene and uneventful, except for the happy travellers who found much to marvel at in the rich colors and design of the interiors and other striking features of the new equipment." Well, let's see, for a moment, just how *much* the free-riders *did* marvel at in-print. *Readers' Guide to Periodical Literature* for 1937–'38, the time that the "freebie" scribes were transported so elegantly to Santa Fe, lists NO *written* coverage of the preview trip!

That dearth of coverage, so it would seem, refuted rather curtly, rather insensitively, *Santa Fe Magazine's* description of its company's first load of preview-passengers as "enthusiastic and keenly interested travelers, among them being many of the best known and most influential newspaper and magazine writers."

A 24-hour turnaround at Chicago for cleaning, re-stocking, and servicing, and *Super-2* was readied for its second goodwill preview, a 2,228-mile run out to the Coast with "a delegation from the Chicago Association of Commerce," a guest list of seventy-two bankers, presidents, vice-presidents, and assorted executive

eminence to people the rolling caravanserais of America's first all-Pullman streamliner.

During *Super-2's* 24-hour turnaround, EMC Diesel No. 2 was released from the plant out at La Grange and, red nose and all, reported for duty. Like any parent, Santa Fe immediately wanted pictures of its newborn so, around 9 o'clock Saturday morning, May 8th, Diesel "2" coupled on to eight cars of *Super-2* and off they went, 25-miles west on the Santa Fe "main" to Lemont, Illinois———lovely, tree-flecked countryside———to pose for sunny portraits by Inland Picture Service (the negatives of which have all been, as so often happens in "big business," lost or destroyed). *Super-2* was, then, in the family album.

Shortly after the first "preview" run, *Super Chief-2* was taken out to a spot near Lemont, Illinois, 26 miles west of Chicago, for publicity photographs. (ABOVE) Many views of the train were taken at this beautiful location with trees gently blowing during the long time exposure to make sure all photographic detail was sharp. On the opposite page, *Super-2* leans into a curve on the same early May afternoon. — BOTH SANTA FE RAILWAY

The smart all-Pullman *Super Chief-2* was an immediate success from its first day of service on the weekly round trip schedule. Passengers had to wait weeks to get confirmation of space. — SANTA FE RAILWAY

7

Once again at 7:00 P.M., May 8th, 1937, the fluted length of *Super-2* car sides stretched, in a panoply of highlights, down the board platform of Dearborn Station's Track 5. Past those cars, walking with a rolling gait, came a thickly-knit man, forty-fivish, with glasses who, when he got to *Oraibi*, handed his bag to the porter and followed him up the steps and on-board that second preview consist. And it was fortunate for those of us who treasure our memories of *Super-2* that he did, because our bespectacled man in the dark suit was that able Midwestern author, David S. Oakes, on-board to write his impressions of *The Super* and the trip West.

In a few minutes, his suitcase tucked away in Bedroom C, Oakes stepped down onto the platform, leaned against a column, and jotted down these words on a yellow legal pad: "The train itself is chastely beautiful and, in the tempered light of early evening, soft shadows sift across the satin sheen of its stainless steel sides. Nothing obtrudes to mar the smooth perspective from the tailored rear of the observation lounge, where shaded lights and mellow colors invite to cozy hours, to the locomotive whose apron pilot and bluntly rounded front somehow resemble the long-visored cap of Jesse Rupe, the engineer, who even now gives expert ear to the drone of the Diesels as he tests their responses to his power-throttle."

7:15, executives all on-board, and Conductor Fred Wanders shouted a peremptory "Boar-r-r-d." Steps folded up-and-in, air hissed, and *Super-2* slid, in Oakes' words, "like a silver serpent, swiftly out of sight." The second preview run was under way and Santa Fe was at it again.

On-board, Oakes and his business and civic *confrères* settled-in, washed, and, if they chose to do so, dressed for dinner in the diner. While dressing, they could have, again had they so desired, watched the May-green countryside of Illinois flash by like an endless movie backdrop, *Super-2's* suspension-system and a jim-dandy roadbed making their ride seem as though it were on a toboggan over new snow.

Again, to quote from the perceptive, contemporary notes of Mr. Oakes on that legal pad: "... and so away to the Harvey Diner where Peter Tausch maneuvers his miracles of meals en route. *Cochiti* is a corridor of pleasant babble as Tausch seats me, among the executives, at a table just forward of the walnut buffet and its overhead peach-tinted mirror. Glancing about, I must commend the carpet's black insets and stripes on a reddish brown field, the flesh colored ceiling, the intermediate harmonies of chocolate-trimmed Bubinga walls, tan drapes, and shades striped in white and pale yellow. To the ceramics lover, I also commend the streamlined silver service and flatware by Mary Elizabeth Jane Coulter ... and the china with her forms, tints, textures, and thirty-seven authentic motifs of ancient Mimbreno Indian pottery."

Voilà, there in Oakes' written *expertise*, you have as good a picturing of *Cochiti* as there is to be had. After dinner, the per-spicacious Oakes wandered back to the next car, and again picking up his legal pad, penned these pithy bits of prose: "Over a 'Corona-Corona' in *Acoma*, the cocktail lounge, one can admire the leaping golden flames in the Ribbon Prima-Vera walls and ceiling, the back bar ornamentation with its central figure of a 'Katchina' inlaid in half-a-dozen rare woods, the black Thunder-bird against the Zebrawood of the bar, and the genuine Navajo rug of red-and-white-and-black above the *écritoire*."

Indeed, the author is ever so pleased that David S. Oakes was aboard *Super-2's* second preview run.

Oakes' notepad had slipped from his sleeping hands and slid

A Budd advertisement in the February 28, 1938 issue of *Newsweek* featured this rendition of the rear section of *Navajo*. The artwork was from a photograph of dark-haired Juliana Romm (seated mid-picture) chatting with Lady Mabel Dunn.

down the rose-colored Pullman blanket onto the floor as writer Juliana Romm walked softly past his door on her way back to the observation lounge in *Navajo*. Ms. Romm, graceful and ineffably lovely, found herself, at last, in the province and care of porter Joseph E. Chapman, thirty-nine years in Pullman service. The dark-haired Ms. Romm, also a note-taker, wrote these lines in a tiny purse notepad: "The name *Navajo* suits this car, this lovely room, so warmly done in sand colored carpeting, copper walls, and turquoise ceiling. The chairs and sofas do, beautifully and faithfully, recapture an original Bayeta blanket and paintings, as though lifted off a pueblo floor, delight my eyes with their charcoal and colored sand faces filling the panels between the windows. Kudos to the designers who have circled a utilitarian air-conditioning soffit with the rainbow which, ordinarily, surrounds three sides of a sand-painting . . . plus plumage of Bluebirds, Red Flickers, Magpies, and Eagles. Beside my chair, set on the wall, their red tips glowing in the half-light, are three-dimensional replicas of the 'Plumed Arrows' customarily the final images in a series of sand-paintings. Yes, I am comfortable, quieted in *Navajo*."

Ms. Romm tossed her dark hair engagingly, folded her notepad, and sought her room in *Taos*, a room she found readied for the night, lighted only by a blue bulb that scarcely did justice to teak paneling and the cocoa-colored upholstery that peeked out from above the bed sheets and blankets. Cradling a cup of icy water in her expressive hands, Ms. Romm sat abed contemplating the darkened scenery, but not for long. Soft and secure in her bed, sleep soon claimed her, dear eyes closed gently.

Super Chief

Super-2 and its sleeping cargo charged across the Illinois flatland, tearing apart little towns with its crimson nose and blaring air horn, sounding incessantly, warning and waking bedded townfolk all along the line. Engineer Jesse Rupe was noted for making-the-time, and that second preview run was to be no exception.

On they went . . . suctioning-up rock ballast off the right-of-way . . . "a raving meteor of sound and mass" was the way passenger-author Christopher Morley expressed it. Morley, one of the few on that preview run who wasn't asleep, loved trains——loved them knowledgeably, the way a Gran Prix driver loves his car. Small wonder, then, that he was lying in the dark with his head propped up on two pillows, staring delightedly out at the careening nightscape from his berth in *Laguna*. Phrases littered his mind, and of that Maytime run, he later wrote . . . "through stations we ripped like tearing a strip of muslin. Villages were blotted out by our frightful howl; they were wiped away, blown behind us!"

Further forward, in a Cypress-lined room in *Isleta*, another non-sleeper on *Super-2*, John Mason Brown, author-lecturer with a "weakness for trains," lay awake too, but unlike Morley, he had his reading light on, pen in hand. Of *Super-2*, Brown wrote . . . "I like it because of the illusion it gives of being miraculously becalmed in the midst of motion. A restful pause in life; a sanctuary on wheels which devours space even as it annihilates time."

Indeed, *Super-2*, on that May 8th night, even at 11:40 P.M., was making and keeping friends. In Diesel "2's" airy cab, Jesse Rupe leaned his chunky bulk forward, rolled his shoulders to loosen tension after 205-minutes without letup at the throttle, and began ever so gently, feeding air into the train lines——— braking, whisper-soft, for the approach to the servicing-track at Shopton.

With Shopton behind it, preview *Super-2* had negotiated the first of 13-stops (58 minutes) that it would make to change engine crews on its way to the Coast . . . 234-miles down; 1,994 to go.

—*Super* CHIEF

When it came to stopping for passenger handling, however, *The Super Chief* was infinitely less expansive than for servicing and changing crews. For her riders, *The Super* paused but four times, briefly, between Chicago and Los Angeles: Kansas City (5-minutes), Barstow (2-minutes), San Bernardino (2-minutes), and Pasadena (2-minutes)———eastbound, the same places in reverse.

Talk of crew changes and passenger stops somehow gives rise to a bit of conjecture. Suppose *The Super's* schedule had called for making the trip in *less* than 39 hours-45 minutes. To have run the train faster, in 1936–'37, would have been to absolutely no avail. She could not have gone head-to-head with aircraft and speeding up, for any reason, would only have roughened the ride, already a rail-burner at "39/45." Moreover, each hour that Santa Fe might have taken off that "39/45" schedule would have put *The Super* into Los Angeles that much earlier than the pre-scribed 9 A.M. arrival, hardly a desirable dividend.

Conversely, slowing down the westbound *Super*, making the journey in, say, "41/45," departing Chicago at 5:15 P.M. instead of 7:15, could have shortened or cut out late business transactions in Chicago, something Santa Fe would not countenance in any way, shape, or form.

"39/45," then, was, despite its occasionally hell-bent pace, the *ideal* schedule for *The Super* to haul its class cargo between ter-minals, and time and operating efficiencies proved it.

Albeit *The Super* ran to an ideally adjusted "39/45" timing, if one viewed things realistically, its departure-time from Chicago was, putting it charitably, an any-time-would-do schedule . . . at

least for its passengers who were coming in from New York on the same day *The Super* left the "Windy City."

The *Broadway Limited* and the *Twentieth Century Limited* out of New York, both rich sources of names for *The Super's* manifest, arrived in Chicago nineish in the morning. *The Super* left Chicago at 7:15 P.M. so, right off the bat, with speedy connections impossible, her passengers from Gotham were confronted with a 10 hour-15 minute layover. It was a boon to the Pump Room but largely a bore to the impatient New York-to-Chicago-to-Hollywood riders.

Even after it was under way, the westbound *Super* got to its second passenger pick-up point, Kansas City, at the unholy hour of 2:12 in the morning! Westbound, then, *The Super* ran in what one almost had to describe as a speedy limbo, merely romping out to the West Coast for mid-morning appointments the day of arrival.

Ah, but *eastbound*, that was where *The Super* really shone! In that direction, she slipped out of Los Angeles-Pasadena about dinner-time, hustled 2,228-miles to a 1:45 P.M. halt at Chicago and, in an hour and forty-five minutes (just time enough for lobster salad and a chilled bottle of *Mardonet '26* at The Blackstone), her New York-bound passengers connected wth *The Broadway* and *The Century*. THAT was convenience . . . time-differentiated, smooth-riding, hard-to-beat convenience!

A new world standard for transcontinental all-Pullman travel was set by *Super-2.* (ABOVE) Racing through the countryside of Keokuk, Iowa, at 90 m.p.h. — E. L. BRANSON (OPPOSITE PAGE) The 8-car *Super-2* dashes through the Illinois countryside. — SANTA FE RAILWAY

Super Chief-2 thunders across the old Canyon Diablo steel viaduct en route to the Coast. — DONALD DUKE COLLECTION

8

Sunday morning, May 9th, 1937, in Colorado, we rejoin the *Super-2* second preview run as it coasts into Trinidad.

Settled in an easy chair in *Navajo*, David Oakes was still jotting on his legal pad and we could, again, do no better than quote from Oakes' handwritten, on-the-scene notes of that 1937 spring day out West: "The *Super Chief* makes only the briefest of operation stops but, here at Trinidad, while a helper engine is attached and the windows are bathed and squeegeed by a lightning fast crew, one can step outside for a full length sight of the train. Its lustre is undimmed for all its race across a thousand miles of plains. At Trinidad, the railroad's really serious business begins and it is the only place where *The Super* welcomes help. Otherwise, the Diesel sees us through unaided.

"2-10-2 No. 925 is our assigned reinforcement and will guide the destinies of the *Super Chief* and its burden of executives up over the crest of Raton Pass. In fifteen miles, we are lifted 1,636 feet to the highest point of our entire journey. Up, up, up toil our titans, puffing and growling in unison, as doggedly persistent as ants dragging a caterpillar.

"As we snake around tortuous turns in the ascent, the view ahead presents an interesting contrast. The steam locomotive fights the grade spectacularly as though to show the newcomer its

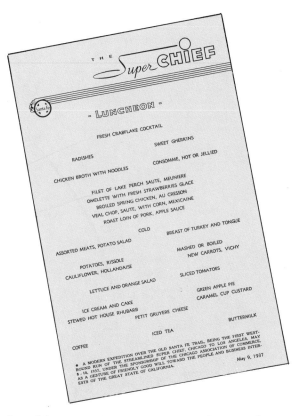

THE _Super_ CHIEF

° LUNCHEON °

FRESH CRABFLAKE COCKTAIL

SWEET GHERKINS

RADISHES

CONSOMME, HOT OR JELLIED

CHICKEN BROTH WITH NOODLES

FILET OF LAKE PERCH SAUTE, MEUNIERE
OMELETTE WITH FRESH STRAWBERRIES GLACE
BROILED SPRING CHICKEN, AU CRESSON
VEAL CHOP, SAUTE, WITH CORN, MEXICAINE
ROAST LOIN OF PORK, APPLE SAUCE

COLD
BREAST OF TURKEY AND TONGUE

ASSORTED MEATS, POTATO SALAD

MASHED OR BOILED
NEW CARROTS, VICHY

POTATOES, RISSOLE
CAULIFLOWER, HOLLANDAISE

SLICED TOMATOES

LETTUCE AND ORANGE SALAD

GREEN APPLE PIE
CARAMEL CUP CUSTARD

ICE CREAM AND CAKE
STEWED HOT HOUSE RHUBARB
PETIT GRUYERE CHEESE

BUTTERMILK

ICED TEA

COFFEE

● A MODERN EXPEDITION OVER THE OLD SANTA FE TRAIL, BEING THE FIRST WEST-
BOUND RUN OF THE STREAMLINED SUPER CHIEF, CHICAGO TO LOS ANGELES, MAY
8 - 10, 1937, UNDER THE SPONSORSHIP OF THE CHICAGO ASSOCIATION OF COMMERCE,
AS A GESTURE OF FRIENDLY GOOD WILL TOWARD THE PEOPLE AND BUSINESS INTER-
ESTS OF THE GREAT STATE OF CALIFORNIA.   May 9, 1937

Life aboard the previewing *Super Chief* was three grand excursions
daily to the dining car for a choice of gratis gourmet delicacies.

fully trained competence; the Diesel follows———willing to accept pointers from an experienced oldster but quietly confident
in its possession of scientific skill.

"In and out weaves this great train———the ring of spectator
mountains remain unmoved before our puny power pageant for
they know we shall pass and they will remain. So it is that they
allow us to ride their backs with impunity. The eye of Raton
Tunnel is threaded and we cross the summit of the pass and, like
a projectile from a gun, we emerge from the tunnel to plunge into
New Mexico. At the far end of the bore, the helper engine, spewing a great exhalation of smoke, cuts off with a final exhaust of
satisfaction. And then we fairly plunge a thousand feet down into
New Mexico to reach Raton, eight miles away.

"But, once again *The Super*, now in the trough, must essay another spiney crest in the backbone of the continent. Ten miles down ere we pass the second line of mountainous defenses which oppose our westward progress. Around the spectacular double horseshoe curve we wind to Ribera on the Pecos River. Down upon us frown the terrific steeps of Glorieta Mesa crowned by Escobas Mountain. Beetling crags, rugged defiles, chilly gusts from snow-mantled summits, a final strain and we glide in swift release down through the granite gash of Apache Canyon——oldest strata of The Rockies——into Lamy. Here ends the Santa Fe Trail, so far as the *Super Chief* is concerned.

"We hurry along through the Pueblo Country beside the winding Rio Grande del Norte. Occasional wisps of smoke betray the adobe dwellings of Indian villages. By the time Albuquerque is reached, approaching dusk enhances the brilliance of the semaphores' fixed stares which have a magnetic quality in the keen air. *The Super's attachés'* white jackets and the gray suits of its executives glimmer about the platform and the torches of the inspectors flicker about the dark recesses beneath the cars.

"Into the panelled warmth of *Cochiti* comes beaming Karl Schwager, co-steward on this special run, to exhibit a brace of trout. They are beauties, caught this morning and taken on board in iced boxes back at La Junta, appearing to weigh about a pound apiece and would make anyone impatient to have them appear even more delectable . . . broiled to perfection."

Oakes, obviously happily, lastingly ensnared by the transitory acumen of the *Super Chief* dining service, labelled his piscine encounter in *Cochiti* a *"coup de maître"* and added this encomium: "The variety and resources of the larder seem inexhaustible and not even a Brillat-Savarin could find less than compliment for the quality and preparation of these viands." Oakes penned this paternally concluding note on Fred Harvey dining: "One learns to accept and savor these blessings over which grace has been shed as well as said."

Second-night-out on *Super-2's* preview run, Diesel No. 2 took the caravaning knights of commerce across the Continental Divide, over the upper reaches of Arizona, through the dusty back washes of California and, in the early morning light, to a gritty halt before the baked brick depot at Barstow to change crews, the last such stop of its kind.

David S. Oakes reveled in any passage over Santa Fe's trackage

Chef Carlos Gardini displays some of the fine foul, meats, wine, and vegetables served aboard the *Super Chief.* This scene was set up for a *Life* Magazine photographer. — GRAPHIC HOUSE

across the San Bernardino mountains————to top them, through Cajon, and make entry to San Bernardino at the bottom. Once more, knowing Oakes' proclivity for Santa Fe's toboggan slide into "Berdoo," suppose we take our last ride with the great old Chicago romantic, up and over The Hill. His notes read ... "Knowing the beguiling stretch ahead, I am in *Cochiti* at 'First Call' for luscious French Toast and steaming coffee as we follow the Cottonwooded course of The Mojave and its sun-tipped wavelets. We climb again for the last effort which will carry us over the San Bernardino and San Gabriel ranges. Joshua trees in infinite variety make their appearance. At Summit, I have my choice of seats in *Navajo* for the spectacle of final flight out of these altitudes, the swift descent toward the coastal plain.

"Here we drop nearly three thousand feet in twenty-five miles. On such a track in such a train, what a thrilling ride it is! It is a crack-the-whip series of turns among beautiful green domes of mountain with glimpses of snow-capped peaks lost and regained as we race through dwarf vegetation where hills fold together and fan out in ever varied formations.

" 'Old Baldy' in his snowy cap uses them as a screen for his game of hide-and-seek with us, sparks of red within the canyon scrub betray the Manzanita, sentinel pines uprear their tousled artistry, and spires of Yucca speak of yesteryear. As we swoop around the turns, the Diesel positively appears to enjoy this home stretch romp. Farther along, ordered orchards appear as we rocket along and finally enter the superb stretch of straight track into San Bernardino.

"From the highway beside us, we receive, with a slight condescension, the hails and farewells of outdistanced motorists. We glide to a cushioned stop in 'Berdoo' and look back, with seemly awe, on the mountain wall and realize how lately we were among its jumbled contours, amazed at man's temerity. Our wheels give off acrid fumes from the heat of recent brake pressures while above us wave the fronds of Washingtonia Palms, for all the world like giant feather dusters thrust into the ground.

SANTA FE FRENCH TOAST

3 slices bread, 3/4-in. thick	1/4 teaspoon salt
4 eggs, slightly beaten	cooking oil
1 cup half and half	confectioners' sugar

Use firm homemade-type of bread. Trim crusts and cut diagonally into triangles. Combine eggs, half and half, and salt. Dip bread in mixture allowing pieces to absorb as much liquid as possible. Fry in about one-half inch cooking oil heated to 325 degrees.

When brown on one side, turn and brown second side. Place on baking sheet and allow to puff in 400 degree oven for 3 to 5 minutes. Drain on paper towels to absorb excess fat. Sprinkle with confectioners' sugar and serve immediately with applesauce, jelly, honey or syrup.

Two young lads watch the arrival of a "preview" run of *Super-2* as it slides into Pasadena on May 10, 1937, bound for Los Angeles. Only local train watchers were aware of its arrival. — ALLEN YOUELL.

"The ride in lovely *Navajo*, from San Bernardino to Los Angeles, packs thrills galore. This is California———truly a realm apart! We bowl along gently. On our left, a straight line of towering Eucalypti gossip softly as we pass. On our right, against a backdrop of mountains, is a marvelous stage set with citrus scenery which stretches from the unfenced right-of-way far up into the foothills.

"Each little town has its packing houses blazoned with trade marks well known everywhere since citrus advertising girdles the civilized world. Now the towns almost run together and bell-alarms are frequent as we cross the wide, palm-lined streets of this paradise of the automobile [even in 1937!]. *The Super Chief's* passage acts as a lodestone for the youngsters who gather on fences and posts to shrill their greetings. The little houses of the suburbs fairly struggle to emerge from wildernesses of geraniums, castor plants, pepper trees, and foliage of infinite variety. Almost suddenly, we slide down another canyon, this one has structural sides, and discover Pasadena.

"Off again, we prepare to take leave of the *Super Chief* special run with genuine regret. It has carried us more than 2,200 miles in full comfort of body and spirit. It has revived the thrills of childhood in a journey and shown us our country in its majesty of miles and manifold aspects. Drifting down from Pasadena, my mind retraces the journey and discovers the stabs of color which marked gay blankets among the Indians clustered on roof-tops of pueblo San Felipe; the marshaled verdancy of the world's greatest vineyard at Cucamonga; the throngs which saluted our arrival everywhere; and many qualities and appointments of the train. In the lap of its creature comforts, surrounded by lavish and diverse beauty, with Peter Tausch and Karl Schwager to plan delights for the inner man while the glorious cavalcade of America's miles marches past my window, I could have lingered longer.

"None less than William Shakespeare, by the way, took the valedictory right out of my mouth when, in 'Henry the Eighth,' he forecast the *Super Chief* with: 'A royal train, believe me.' ———But, . . . here is Los Angeles."

Another "preview" run arrives at La Grande Station in Los Angeles on May 10, 1937. Once the passengers have detrained, a brakeman prepares to uncouple the locomotive from its train. The Road Foreman of Engines leans from the cab for the "all clear." Once received, engineer Galard Slonaker gives two blasts on the air horn and inches his powerful diesels toward the roundhouse at Redondo Junction. — RALPH MELCHING

9

The last thousand yards or so of the Santa Fe's mainline into Los Angeles, in 1937 anyway, used to wander along behind a succession of packing plants, warehouses, and factories up on the west bank of the deep-sunken but usually bone-dry Los Angeles River. It was anything but an imposing entrance to "Hollywoodland" but, for better or worse, it was the weed-strewn right-of-way path that David Oakes and the executives riding the *Super-2* preview run looked out on that hazy-sunny morning of May 10th, 1937.

Galard Slonaker, a fine engineer and a friend, working the brake valve like the artist he was, spotted the First Street Bridge ahead and flipped on the bell switch to toll chimey warnings ———" 'ning, 'ning, 'ning, 'ning." Headlight gleaming lemonish, road dust obscuring its crimson-and-yellow hood, Slonaker drove road-weary Diesel No. 2 and *Super-2* beneath that bridge and rumbled past a noisy crowd of several thousand crammed onto the platform of time-stained La Grande Station———all decked out in festive red-white-and-blue bunting to welcome the spanking new Budd train on its first arrival in Los Angeles.

The wheels were covered with sand———even bits of tumbleweed———as the cars brushed hotly by the milling faces and caused the semi-circles of colored muslin on the eaves to flutter

Some of the throng standing before bunting-draped La Grande Station to "welcome" *Super Chief-2* to Los Angeles for the very first time on the sunny morning of May 10, 1937.

in their wake. Air pressure exhaled from brake cylinders to scatter bits of paper across the asphalt paving. With a final heavy sigh, the corrugated length of *Super-2* came to a stop and stood shimmering in the warm morning sun, heat waves dancing off its highlighted skin. Doors banged open and folded stairs dropped down out of their ribbed receptacles, spilling more desert dirt out of corners to form little piles along the rails.

Pullman porters in their white jackets exited first, wiping the curved hand rails, and then positioned their yellow "one steps" below the bottom stairs.

Preceded by advance men, the cargo of executives, led by Santa Fe head man Bledsoe, stepped hesitantly into the jumble of strange faces pressed in the shadow of *Super-2*. Salty old John McCutcheon, white-haired, hollow-cheeked editorial cartoonist for the Chicago *Tribune*, peered mischievously into the sea of faces and, with his cane pointing the way, led the *entourage* up three steps and onto a wooden, flag-draped speakers' stand, vital *accoutrement* for welcomings in the Thirties.

Bending his tall, sparse frame to a KFI microphone, Mc-Cutcheon said, without preamble of any kind, "The Super Chief gave me super speed, super service, and super comfort." With that, the same economy of expression that typified his cartoons, the Dean of American cartoonists plopped a gray fedora on his bald head and sat down.

Charles Dawes, Vice President under Coolidge, chirped "Hello" and went on to opine, "It's a shame all public speakers aren't limited to thirty seconds." No, it wasn't memorable rhetoric but, keep in mind, train-arrivals weren't the spawning grounds of valid oratory. *Super-2's* was no exception.

After a spate of Chicago executive eulogia, an NBC announcer, cupping his hand behind one ear, succumbed to ether-borne rapture and likened *Super-2* to a "necklace of pearls." That ended the ceremonies, as well it should!

President Samuel Bledsoe of the Santa Fe Railway (midway down the stairs at the left), leads his guests off *Super-2* and into the bright Southern California morning, May 10, 1937, at La Grande Station.

At the south end of the depot, Slonaker inched his Diesels away from the cars, gave two short blasts on the horn, revved up the engines, and moved off briskly toward the roundhouse.

The executives were, by that time, perspiring freely and, accordingly, more than ready to abandon their wooden folding chairs and retreat to the dimly lighted coolness of the sandstone waiting room for icy glasses of fresh orange juice. Refreshed and revived, the newly arrived Association of Commerce guests piled into automobiles waiting out on Santa Fe Avenue and were whisked away for six days on the town beginning with luncheon at MGM. Oh yes, Santa Fe could, indeed, make one feel welcome.

The crowd back on the platform hovered around *The Super*, straining for glimpses into the cars but, for the moment, had to be content with looking up at ceilings, rubbing admiring hands over the fluted stainless sides, or strolling back to the curved end of *Navajo* for wistful glances at the purple name sign, its circular glass face hurriedly wiped free of dust by a prideful brakeman.

The crowd dispersed and, except for the sound of flapping bunting material, the old depot fell silent or as nearly silent as a depot can be. A yard engine came for the *Super-2* cars and, as it coupled on, portly agent Myer Mendelsohn pushed a young man up the open stairwell and into *Navajo*. The eight cars edged out of La Grande and, as *Navajo's* end window slipped past, a delighted wave greeted Mendelsohn, just this writer's happy acknowledgement of the agent's sanctuarial alliance.

On south, along the river, *Super-2*, trailing its smokily aspirating engine, pinged over street crossings and behind a panorama of small factories, passed Olympic Boulevard and, shortly, slid onto the "Y" at Washington Boulevard. From the "Y," it was back up into the Eighth Street Coach Yard and, at last, rest.

With *Super-2* in the yard, now would seem to be an appropriate time to tell the uninitiated reader something about what was done to the transcontinental flyer after it got to the Coast.

In anticipation of its new streamliner, Santa Fe laid nearly six-hundred feet of track up on 8x12-inch timbers which, when one adds up the inches of timbers, track, and wheels, gave workmen about 5′8″ head room under the cars. That allowed greater access to train equipment, so much of which was, of necessity, tucked away, esthetically, underneath, behind the ribbed skirting that was not movable.

By accident, surely not design, the added elevation set the line of the car floors at about eye level and dramatized, to a marked degree, the image of the streamlined *Super-2*, lent it the majesty of height, something resembling the low-angle perspectives so dear to the hearts of architects and artists.

No sooner had the yard engine pulled *Super-2* up on the work track and set the brakes than gangs of workmen converged on the cars. They clambered on top of them, under them, and inside them to probe their darkest recesses and cabineted utilities with flashlights and the omnipresent yellow-handled screwdrivers. They read the bad-order cards which outlined problems such as "flat" wheels, cracked axles, broken air hoses, defective brakes . . . things that would affect the cars' ability to make the next trip. Their practiced eyes could and did diagnose, in short order, the wear-and-tear that *Super-2* had suffered on its roaring dash across 2,200 miles of prairie, mountain, and blanched desert.

The first order of business at Eighth Street was to set wooden wedges under the leading and trailing edges of the wheels and hang a "blue flag" on a grab-iron at the end of *Navajo*. Next, two men, both in knee-boots, scurried up ladders and onto the car roofs and, with one spraying water from a garden hose and the other wielding a mop-brush dunked in a bucket of "Oakite" acid-wash, the two, starting at the head end, began wetting down, washing, and rinsing off the lengthy expanse of ribbed stainless steel.

Another gang, on the ground, also with hoses and buckets of "Oakite," attacked the road dirt with long-handled brushes—the kind that, back in the Thirties, were used to lay-up and paste posters on billboards. Even the 194 windows were squeegeed by hand!

After what must seem, by today's standards, arduously primitive methods, the hand-washing was done, but be assured by one who was there often and saw it close-up, *Super-2* in its sparkling hand-burnished coat was worth all the effort.

Washed and rinsed, *Super-2* sat and air-dried herself 'til along came a masked-and-goggled painter pulling a compressor in a two-wheel hand cart. From the thin hoses, he sprayed the trucks and what underbody was not hidden by the side skirts with a fresh coat of aluminum paint, casting a striking sheen over springs, journals, and bolsters———artfully pulling together the eight cars into what seemed a single lustrous tube. With the outer shell seen to, on-board yard men prodded and poked into electrical lockers, motor casings, cylinder housings, and the panoply of fuses, switches, armatures, piping, and circuitry that surrounded, interlaced, and animated the seemingly uncontrived car-lengths of *Super-2*. Bulky bags of soiled bed linen were heaved out of vestibules to form a careless rank of snowy bundles. Sleeping berths were opened and fumigated, carpets vacuumed, bed lamps polished, toilets disinfected, wash basins scoured, carafes refilled, sills dusted, and 194 windows washed all over again.

The interminable housekeeping continued. Wooden carts piled high with the woven residue of 2,200 miles and seventy passengers were trundled off to the Pullman laundry up at the north end of the ancient brick yard-buildings. Batteries were recharged, stove tops got a hand-scouring with pumice blocks, broiler racks lost their blackness from assiduous wire brushings, air-conditioning vent-covers were removed and brushed free of dust and, by late afternoon, the residual odors of lazing humans and their anatomical wear-and-tear had all but dissipated and the cars took on an air of almost pristine clarity.

The dinnertime exodus of yard crews left *Super-2* all but deserted, peopled only by an occasional coveralled car "tonk" who clanked through to check on one of the multitude of working parts peculiar to those seven passenger cars.

Super-2, bathed, primped, and fussed over to a fare-thee-well, was about to spend the first night of what ordinarily would have been a 35-hour layover in Los Angeles. On that preview run, however, she was slated for a longer stay and due for exhibit the next three days (two at La Grande Station and one at San Diego). With that in mind, the yard crews had truly outdone themselves and, standing on its raised track in a yard populated with nothing save dark green, heavyweight coaches and Pullmans, *Super-2* appeared almost to exult in her solitary, luminous elegance.

10

T *he Super's* May 10th, 1937 had been a hectic day, and
the three ahead promised the greatest concentration of
guests on-board that she would ever know: the pressures
of a good many thousand feet tramping her corridors and rooms
during three open-house introductions to a 1937 public that
loved new trains.

Still, hectic though her hours had been up 'til then, *Super-2's*
day wasn't over yet. She had another social commitment: a 7:30
P.M. on-board dinner for the Los Angeles press.

Around "five," a Diesel switcher came to Eighth Street for the
cars and lumbered up the ramped track to couple on. Wedges
were pulled from under the wheels, the "blue flag" lifted off
Navajo, brakes hissed in release, and the serpentine of shiny
stainless eased away from its berth to thread its way through col-
umns of coaches and aged yard-buildings and drift to a stop beside the also-aged Fred Harvey Commissary under the Seventh
Street Bridge.

Two four-wheeled carts, laden to overflowing with comestibles,
potables, munchables———anything edible that might fill, gentle, sate, or surfeit the newsmen destined to partake of that
mobile cornucopia———were disgorged into *Cochiti's* kitchen for
the upcoming introductory culinary *fête.*

The Fred Harvey Commissary at Los Angeles became the gathering place for the choicest foods and produce. In this scene, victuals are being loaded aboard dining car *Cochiti* through the outside kitchen door. — GRAPHIC HOUSE

Stepping nimbly around, over, and between bags, boxes, and bottles that clogged the kitchen's aisles and counters, Chef Carlos Gardini and his white-aproned aides had the stoves and broiler fired up and set for cooking in what seemed, to this writer, mere seconds.

Snaking along the riverbank, *Super-2* traced her way into La Grande Station and, about "six," stopped just south of the waiting room. Smoke fluttered from the diner chimneys and *Cochiti* presented a brightly lighted scene of bustle. Fresh flowers appeared at every window, vivid petalled accompaniment to the African Rosewood walls.

By 6:30, the dinner-hour set to accommodate late evening deadlines of the *Examiner* and *Times,* reporters and feature writers began arriving at La Grande in a steady but far from orderly procession of cabs, roadsters and, if memory serves the author correctly, a few via clattering, clanging No. "9" streetcars. Some of the scribes had, it was fragrantly obvious, already taken precautionary measures to ward off the hazard of riverfront chilling and thus, came teetering on the scene, florid-faced and breathing heavily.

The newshawks were met at the steps of *Oraibi's* vestibule by that innate greeter and friend to the film folk, rotund Myer Mendelsohn who, with his assistant, "Red" Proctor, handed each guest a brown-black-and-white fold-out pamphlet illustrating the interiors he would be seeing soon after "dinner in the Diner."

Once on-board, the Fourth Estaters turned right and into *Cochiti,* where they were met by two other glad-handing jewels in Santa Fe's crown of people-pleasers, omnipresent dining steward Peter Tausch, and LA public relations chief Ed Ryder. There was one thing, beside running damned fine trains, that Santa Fe

Super-2's diner ***Cochiti*** in the Eighth Street Coach Yard in Los Angeles. The kitchen section is located on the opposite side of the car. — STAN KISTLER

129

Chef Carlos Gardini trims fat from a Prime Rib Roast before it is placed in the oven and made ready for the evening meal. — GRAPHIC HOUSE

could do with unequalled flourish: that was put on a "spread," and that May 10th night, they were in fine fettle for entertaining. Armed with their legendary voraciousness and Mary Coulter's primitive-design silverware, the "ink-stained" guests tucked the Irish damask napkins in their shirtfronts and began, forthwith, to diminish and demolish Chef Gardini's lavish feast, the details of which still appear, jotted amongst the conjugations of French verbs in the author's high school notebook in now-fading ink-well ink . . .

Cold Consomme or Crab-Flake Cocktail

———

Roast Ribs of Prime Beef or Broiled Spring Chicken

———

Potatoes Rissole or Persilade

———

Sliced Tomatoes and Watercress

———

Gâteaux et Glacés - Green Apple Pie

———

Petit Gruyère Cheese

———

Coffee and Liquers
Vins

Angel Blanc '34   *Oiseau-mouche Rouge '31*

Slabs of finely-marbled prime rib rode in from *Cochiti's* ovens in a majestic pink procession and plump chickens, still sizzling and brownly criss-crossed from the broiler rack, came to savory halts before the hungry media men. Wine flowed and conversation diminished from boisterous prattle to rapturous mumblings.

Just outside *Cochiti*, in a station office sweetened by the ingrained fragrances of good cigars and coal smoke, the author enjoyed the same meal as the press people, only off a tray that the Pickwickian Mendelsohn had spirited out to him————piping hot 'neath two damask napkins————to be eaten joyously at the old agent's littered roll-top desk. No one, but no one, even in *Cochiti's* glamorous setting, wined and watched over, could have been happier than that eighteen-year-old seated at that battered roll-top. The memory of it is still fresh, still sweet————as sweet as the dish of thick, *real* cream ice-cream that topped off that *Super* dinner at La Grande, May 10th, 1937.

131

Around ten o'clock, the last knot of newsmen roistered out of *Cochiti*, hollered "Good nights" to Myer, and headed, we assumed, back to city rooms to confront recalcitrant typewriters and, on those old "mills," bang-out glowing copy on their visits to *Super-2*, copy that would mirror their hard-bitten delight, approval anyway, of what they had seen and eaten and admired.

Oddly enough, we will never know *what* Los Angeles' newsmen thought of their luscious dinners or, for that matter, *how* they reacted to their tours through the cars of *Super-2*. Not a word of copy appeared in the city papers to mark the occasion!

Suffice to say, there was no food left. The wine was gone and the ash trays were filled with crumpled cigarette packs, pipe-knockings, and cold cigars. *Super-2* had been inspected alright, but somehow it didn't rate press coverage. All that *did* appear was a handsome ad that Santa Fe ran to invite the public on-board *The Super* on the 11th and 12th of May. Yes, the ad was run.

Dishevelled and needing her makeup freshened, it was back to the coach yard for *Super-2*. Her seats and couches were strewn with mimeographed press-releases; the diner showed spills and cried out for the crumb tray. Down to Eighth Street, then, for a late night re-do and spiffying for its upcoming dates with the public . . . the old best-foot-forward approach in action.

Tucked-in again at the yard, the racket of green-bagged vacuums and the scraping of pumice stones on *Cochiti's* stove-tops and broiler echoed from within the cars. *The Super* was having her neck scrubbed and, by that time, even a dyed-in-the-wool *Super devotée* like the author was tired out from a long day in and around the train. Appropriately, he headed south in the darkness, walking beside the San Diego "main" toward Olympic Boulevard to catch a "J" trolley.

A last look from the Olympic bridge trolley-zone offered *Super-2's* glossy veneer mirroring the yellow yard lights all the way back to the observation car, where a blue lantern flickered brightly to mark the rounded tail of *Navajo*, in whose end window a goatskin-shaded lamp glowed warmly. A "Diego" steam local, running a little late, flashed by and flung a cloud of smoke over the scene and, from out of the white pall, sent back the mournful mezzo of its chime whistle as a postlude to the panorama of black ranks of inert car bodies settled in for the long night.

132

Super-2 was up early on the 11th to go meet its visitors and stood parked in front of La Grande depot by "nine." That ancient restraint, rope, was strung about ten feet out from the car faces, one end to the other, to channel the "eager crowds" which were, as Santa Fe said, "anticipated."

Inside *Super-2* at La Grande that May morning, to prevent dawdling or sampling, clothesline was strung across sections, stateroom doors, dining car chairs, and the furniture in lounge car *Acoma*. The placation of public viewing was one thing; wear-and-tear on the furniture was quite another. In other words, the spectators would go through only five of the seven cars (*Isleta* and *Laguna* were "twins," so there was no need to open both of them).

The visitors would, therefore, board the train through the rear door of *Isleta*, pass through the curtained stillness of *Laguna*, walk the lengths of lounge and diner *Acoma* and *Cochiti*, continue into and out of the corridors of all-bedroom cars *Oraibi* and

Observation car *Navajo* and its curved galleria on-exhibit at La Grande Station on May 12, 1937. Viewing-ramp on the right gave the public a look "inside".

Taos, and get off at the door to *Navajo.* From there, those who wished to could mount a six-foot long, three-foot high ramp positioned alongside the first big window at the end of *Navajo.*

From that ramp, one could have a peek into the sacrosanct Indian-lounge of the observation car. Had the lines of people been routed into *Navajo,* surely, considering its uniqueness, traffic would have collected, perhaps even clotted, at the round rear end. Thus it was decided to by-pass that loveliest of all the cars and, as a gesture of appeasement, provide the ramp at the window.

By "ten," the crowds, as anticipated, were on board and starting through *Super-2.* All day long, the curious trudged along the canvas runners, trying as best they could to fill their eyes with the *panache* of woods, colors, and fabrics which were so appealingly set before them. Up until "five," the procession of eager faces flowed, in and out of the cars, creating a sedate Conga-line of murmurous admiration———admiration that, though it is repetitive to say so, would bring few, if any, of the admirers into the perfumed *purlieux* of *The Super Chief,* No. 2 or any other numerical designation of the train.

In the latter days of The Depression, it cost a then-princely $97 to ride *The Super* to Chicago in a lower berth———$110 in a double bedroom! To the majority of viewers on board *Super-2* that May 11th, $97 represented a month or more of hard-earned salary. But exposure, in Santa Fe's eyes, synonymized good will and in 1937, good will was translated into a rare and precious commodity to the people-seeking railroads of the country.

At "five," *Isleta's* doors closed and the last sprinkling of sightseers headed inside the new *Super* to emerge, minutes later, at the foot of the ramp beside *Navajo.* The train was locked, and a yard crew took up the dirtied lengths of canvas, laid fresh runners, turned out the lights, and left *Super-2* to spend the night nestled beside the brick walls of old La Grande, readied for more of the same the following day.

Wednesday, the 12th, *Super-2* met another swarm of admirers in its seven-hour open house, and aging La Grande reverberated with the babble of more people than it had ever hosted since it opened, forty-four years before, at First and Santa Fe. Wednesday night, after a gnawing, hectic day, the new cars were washed, dusted, tidied, and re-stocked with fine foods and beverages for a next-day run southward.

Thursday, the 13th, and *Super-2* was once more at the La Grande platform, that morning to entrain President Bledsoe and a covey of railroad "notables." By 9:03 they had negotiated the tracks through the freight yard south of the depot, taken the "main," and scurried off toward San Diego for lunch.

After the noonday repast for the big, near big, and people of means, the new streamliner's doors swung open to the public. By 9 P.M. more than 13,000 "fascinated" folk had shuffled through *Super-2*, a thumping viewing-audience for the not yet inaugurated Train of the Stars. Crowds who couldn't be accommodated on-board milled around the car perimeters all day, some taking snapshots of the fluted flyer, even in that aspect of design, one of a kind. The picture-takers were, by the way, lucky, for that *Super Chief* would never again enter San Diego.

In that week of May 10th, while the *Super-2* cars had been the cynosure of most eyes, two stainless-clad Diesel locomotives ———one unit with the crimson "nose"———had waited, off stage, at the roundhouse in Los Angeles 'til called upon to head up the junket to San Diego. There at the power end of *The Super*, idling in that distinctive guttural mumble, the brand new Electro-Motive E 1A tandem, boasting sufficient credentials in *puissance*, speed rating, and air-smooth styling to lure even the most miscreantic '37 steam enthusiast to their side, began, on that May 13th afternoon, to attract their own following.

Even today, forty-two years after *Super-2's* afternoon in San Diego, in places like Milwaukee and in hearts like David Morgan's, one still finds misty-eyed faithfulness to EMC's E 1A "clan." The first lightweight *Super Chief*, then, not only captured hearts with its once-in-a-lifetime passenger car lineup, but it also overtured an attractive, inimitably colored, and remarkably long-lived Diesel duo to launch those cars across a showcase system.

While *Super-2* and its new Diesels were down at San Diego, *Super-1*———behind 1 and 1-A and a *third* Diesel unit———on its last-run-ever to the Coast, slid quietly into Los Angeles, had its seven cars bathed, and settled back at Eighth Street waiting to make the return trip———its final trip anywhere as a train ———to Chicago the next day, May 14th. Things were of-the-moment at Santa Fe and *Super-1* was, therefore, on its way out . . . eastbound and westbound.

Super-2, a rousingly successful twenty-four hour sojourn with

the public at San Diego under its belt, rolled———almost pranced———to a smart stop at La Grande about noon, the 14th, to let off a covey of seventy "business leaders and newspaper representatives" from the Silver City. Santa Fe's house organ termed the trip a "goodwill tour" to Los Angeles "for the purpose of inspecting firsthand the reputed comforts and unusual appointments of this most modern train." What the "business leaders" and their newspaper companions thought of the train, the trip, or Los Angeles is lost to us, their reactions———unspoken and unwritten———floating uncapturable in the far reaches of limbo.

Free of its businessmen and media cargo, the cars of *Super-2* headed for the omnipresent Eighth Street coach yard and the E 1A Diesels settled in at the roundhouse, right next to 1 and 1-A and an infrequent visitor to Redondo Junction, that "third" Diesel mentioned previously. Cars and Diesels, if, in fact, mechanical inanimates can "think," pondered the next day-and-a-half, roughly speaking, as well they might, considering what those hours would mean to all of them.

Eight o'clock on the night of the 14th, *Super-1*, in what the author has always considered an inglorious end to a great old train (and that's really what it was———old, like an aging diva), tossed its head back, ignored the nearly empty "house" at La Grande Station, and made its way out of the also aging depot . . . flaunting the still-handsome purple insignia on its observation railing in proud *adieu* to the mere handful of faithful there to see its farewell exit. Odd, isn't it, that the seven heavy cars and two bull-necked Diesels didn't inspire wider devotion? *C'est la vie.*

Samuel Thomas Bledsoe studied law at the University of Texas and, after being admitted to the bar, became Santa Fe's local attorney at Ardmore, Oklahoma. He then rose rapidly through the legal department to become president, May 2, 1933. Under Bledsoe, who took over in a depression period, the Santa Fe expanded through the hard times. He built the road's fleet of streamliners, ten for transcontinental runs, and five for interstate runs. The first run of *Super-2* was a "present" on his 68th birthday and he and Mrs. Bledsoe made the trip.

11

Saturday, the 15th of May, 1937, saw the usual flurry that surrounded departures of big-name trains forty years ago but, most likely, it was a 4:30-5:00 P.M. radio broadcast over Los Angeles' KNX-KFWB that really started the day off. Walter Huston, great old film and stage actor, drew the featured role on the program which was called———somewhat grandly, to be sure, but still with commendable directness———"The Saga of the Santa Fe." It was, so the *Santa Fe Magazine* explained, "Dedicated to the Super Chief, its inauguration and history-making achievement."

With more verve than script-quality, Huston———a seasoned train rider from the hurly-burly days of split-week vaudeville ———warmed to the task and, in spite of the loudpedal that was put on Santa Fe "builders and pioneers," not *The Super*, the old trouper pumped a lot of life into that half-hour that, today, we would scarcely call "prime time." At least, the Los Angeles radio audience knew *The Super* was due out that night, and by 7:00 P.M., five thousand people———not all of them listeners, to be sure———descended on La Grande and turned what was generally considered by most people———not imbued with station-fancying———a desultory pile of Arabic brick work into a miniature Tower of Babel.

This advertisement appeared on the radio page of the *Los Angeles Times* for May 15, 1937, informing the listening public of the first eastbound run of the new *Super Chief-2.*

Super-2 looked radiant as it loomed over the packed *bon voyage* platform, reminding the author of something out of a giant Erector set. The passengers for that "Special Good Will Run" ———a term that, by that time in Santa Fe's two-weeks of "preview-running" *Super-2*, had become almost morbidly overused ———were the by-then familiar seventy "business and cultural leaders." The "seventy" and, in some instances, their ladies, were safely aboard and already lounging in French silk robes by A. Sulka, puffing "Murad" cigarettes, and scanning copies of *Forbes* and *Business Week.*

Up at the business end of *Super-2*, idling off a fine mist of exhaust, stood a trio of Diesels: the new-to-the-road duo that were numbered "2" and an out-of-uniform compatriot, "512." "512," boxy and squarish, even more squarish than 1 and 1-A, was a widely-travelled Electro-Motive demonstration unit that, along with its twin, "511," had carried the gospel of non-articulated Dieseling to a good many corners of a good many unconverted railroads.

"512," a hardy old brute, was hooked up to the bright-and-shiny "2" for just what one would expect: to put its two-year-old,

140

sweat-stained, 1,800 h.p. shoulder into the bedevilling grades of Santa Fe's western half and, with the total package of 5,400 h.p. that its presence provided, vault *Super-2* over-the-top and on to the flatlands where she could burn rail into Chicago.

Santa Fe, you could bet, had plans for that eastbound run of *Super-2*, and those plans wouldn't be thwarted by insufficient power! "512" was Santa Fe's ungainly internal combustion insurance policy against any such an eventuality.

To handle the first leg of that "special" run, Santa Fe put a couple of real runners in "2's" cab: Engineer Bert Wallace and his "go-get-'em" fireman, Rex Clayton. There'd be no tomfoolery from Los Angeles to Barstow with those two driving and the road knew it. At that moment, however, Wallace wasn't in the cab, but rather, standing below the cab door signing autographs. Yes, autographs, because in those gentler days when everything wasn't tinged with "cool," an engineer was a larger-than-life figure, the "747" pilot of his time. Kids, real and reverted, dreamed of running an engine, and any one of them there at La Grande that Saturday night would have given his eyeteeth to be taking *that* run to Chicago!

Back along the cars, Vuitton luggage and battered Gladstone bags were piled on board and the staterooms of the few women passengers came alive with the color and fragrance of bouquets and bunches of cut flowers. A cart with a smattering of wardrobe trunks jouncing on it rattled toward the baggage car. Obscuring the asphaltic rattle of that cart were the voices of the USC Glee Club Choir, a sound so pleasant and so foreign to the sooty atmosphere of La Grande.

The crowd was pretty evenly distributed over La Grande's tarmac and along the 642-foot length of *Super-2*: so many by the cars———ogling the "celebs;" a goodly number at the rear of *Navajo*———intrigued by its sign and the colorful interiors they could see through the windows; and, to be sure, a sizeable gathering up by the Diesels.

In a green autograph book, eagerly proffered and pressed into his hand, Engineer Wallace penned one more signature and pulled a worn-smooth Elgin out of the pocket of his white coveralls. Noting the time, 7:55, he edged away from the encircling autograph-seekers. "Gotta go now," he said in that almost-courtly way of his———smiling the warm Wallace smile——— and, with just a trace of the dramatic, made his way up the side-

141

ladder and into the cab. "Next time," he shouted out the window half-apologetically to those whose books he hadn't gotten around to signing. The onlookers were delighted and chorused back, "See ya next trip!"

From inside the cab came the piercing "sooo-weet" of the conductor's signal, the "Highball," and almost in one motion, Wallace flicked the bell valve, snapped on the headlamp to "bright," released the train brake and the engine brake, throttled out, and eased forward.

The bell instantly drove most of the head-end crowd back and away from the three Diesels, and the sudden flash of the headlight scattered the rest of them. The 5400 "horses" roaring to life———spouting sparks and blue exhaust from the stacks——— sent admiring shivers through most of the five-thousand watchers. As Wallace throttled "2" and "512" smoothly from the starting "runs," *Super-2's* 385-tons rolled ever faster past the envying figures who waved unacknowledged waves to the smug faces glancing condenscendingly from cozy stateroom windows.

By the time the observation car *Navajo* hustled by, a brakeman———leaning out of the vestibule door———waved his lantern with the lordly disdain of a Bourbon Royalist scorning the thronging "revolutionists" in the *Place de la Concorde*. The crowning touch of that May 15th *Super-2* departure from Los Angeles was when her lighted purple sign shot beneath the First Street Bridge and curved away to be swallowed up by the blackness . . . its hurrying flight marked only by the fading tones of the air horn drifting back to a by-then silencing La Grande.

On up along the riverbank she maneuvered, across the bridge, and past Lincoln Heights Jail, into Highland Park, through the "cut" at old South Pasadena Station, along Fair Oaks, and into the corridor from Glenarm on north the few blocks to Pasadena Station, where W. K. Etter and a few other Santa Fe "brass" who lived in San Marino boarded *Super-2*.

In no time at all, *Super-2* was snaking its way past the City Hall and into Santa Fe's "back alley" right-of-way that runs behind row upon row of neatly-tended, flower-bowered California bungalows and eastward to a "race-track" stretch through the east San Gabriel Valley, where they would roar by Azusa, Pomona, and by all means, Cucamonga (the town made famous by "train announcer" Mel Blanc on the old Jack Benny radio-show when it came out . . . "kuke- - - - - -a-mung-guh").

142

Appropriately, Blanc and the Benny troupe were regulars on *The Super* and quite often, the older ones of us will remember, devoted entire half-hours to imaginary trips aboard Santa Fe's pride-and-joy.

Super Chief-2's Diesel-electric locomotives on display along Exposition Boulevard, across the street from the University of Southern California's many-windowed School of Dentistry.

12

By the time the "business and cultural leaders" were at-table for that May 15th, 1937 first-night-out dinner, *Super-2* was better than five-minutes early into San Bernardino and it was transparently obvious to all but the rankest novitiates in the passenger-list what Santa Fe had in store for this last uncarded *Super* run. In a few words, *a flat-out record run———wire to wire!* How fast no one had said but, using the 60-mile Los Angeles—San Bernardino leg as a yardstick, and if that speed was maintained, *Super-2* would be knocking one minute off the regular schedule every 12.38-miles.

Well, time would tell but, even as *Super-2* sailed out of "Berdoo," one could feel Wallace pouring the "coal" to the Diesels, and the train wheels seemed to "bite" into the rails for that extra bit of traction. Putting their backs into the climb up Cajon, the E 1A's and "512" roared in and out of sandstone cuts, spewed their oily stack fumes onto clumps of canyon brush, and mounted Summit with a confident growl and two sharp "blats" that Wallace snapped out of the air horn to the dispatcher up there on the "hill."

Super-2 literally rambled downhill to Victorville, shot past the yellow-frame depot and, as the cars bent to the curves at Helendale, was doing a "hundred" and gathering speed under Wallace's

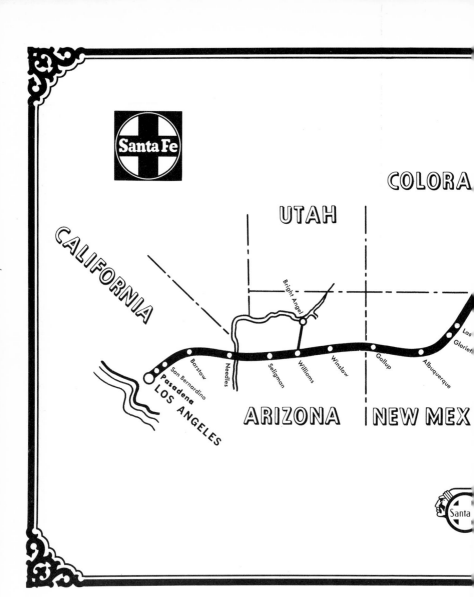

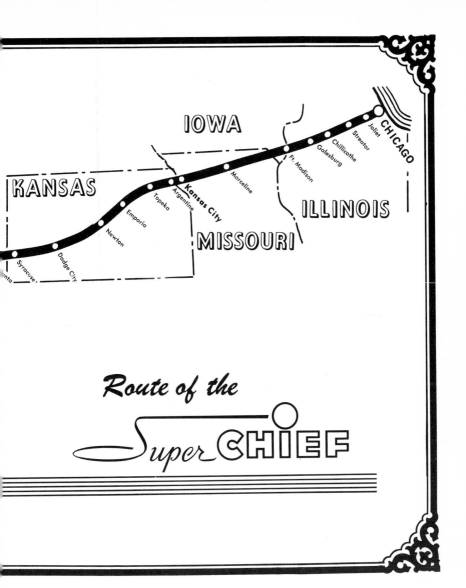

Route of the **Super CHIEF**

The primary purpose of the *Super Chief* was to save hours of time between Chicago and Los Angeles — the fast record was accomplished with no sacrifice of comfort — nor compromise with luxury. The *Super* covered many sections of its route in better than mile a minute speeds. It regularly covered 202.4 miles of its eastbound run between La Junta and Dodge City in exactly 145 minutes, or, including the time necessary for acceleration, slow-downs and deceleration, at an average speed of 83.8 m.p.h. Between Dodge City and Newton, a distance of 153.1 miles, the *Super* covered the distance in 122 minutes, or 75.3 m.p.h. Never before had the world seen such fast land travel.

The dining car steward serves a passenger a grilled Rocky Mountain Trout. (ABOVE RIGHT) Second cook Herman Sirio about to slice a turkey. — SANTA FE RAILWAY

slick, pick-up-your-feet-and-go throttling. Braking to a creamy stop beside the service "plugs" at Barstow, Wallace's Elgin read 11:02:30 (2½-minutes ahead of schedule) and, back in the cars, not a drink had been spilled nor a meld of cards nudged off a table. *Super-2* was 141-miles into the run and so far, not even breathing hard.

Its windshield wiped, undercarriages checked, and a fresh engine crew in the cab, the trio of Diesels accelerated a throaty, echoing exit past the red brick depot, between the hills that ringed the yard, and bore into the Mojave for a night of desert running.

Seven-thirty the next morning found *Super-2* hurrying along just east of Cliffs, Arizona, road foreman Lee Pearson at the throttle, flinging the miles of red earth behind her———44-minutes to the good———time achieved principally by dint of Pearson's working the free-wheeling "notches" and keeping a hummingbird's touch on the brake valve. In other words, letting 'er roll!

The waking celebrities were, for the most part, circulating, and when the chimes sounded "first call for breakfast," the sunny diner filled rapidly with Oxford gray, blue pin-stripes and, as already suggested, a large floral print here and there. *Pince-nez* sprouted around the car, the better to peruse *Super-2's* un-purfled card-menus and, although most of the passengers were new to Harvey fare, it wasn't long 'til word got around: "Order the French toast; it's dee-lish-us." And so it was, pan-fried first and then baked golden-brown to an altitude of several inches and served, piping hot, beneath a snowfall of powdered-sugar.

The creator of most of those French toast orders, chef Eddie Dyke, stood before a crowded stove in *Cochiti's* pitching kitchen bumping-out lighter-than-air omelettes, marking and garnishing them into things of the purest fluffy delight. For Alan Hale Sr., Dyke concocted his omelette with a robust, made-from-scratch Creole sauce topped with a special garnish of alternating "dia-

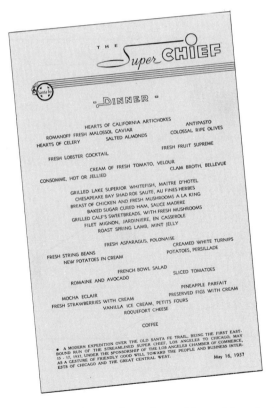

Dinner menu for the first eastbound run of the stainless steel *Super-2* on May 16, 1937.

monds" of green pepper and pimento. For a just-cooked *sweet* omelette, Dyke would sprinkle a layer of granulated sugar on top and then, using a red-hot spoon handle that he had thrust in an open flame, he'd sear a pattern of diagonal criss-crosses into that sugared topping. Plopping plump cherries or strawberries into the browned scorings, he'd send the four-egg gem on its way ————nestled in parsley————to the one lucky enough and knowledgeable enough to have ordered that happy piece of cookery. A Dyke *Super* omelette was, indeed, a treat not to be forgotten!

Super-2 romped into Winslow at 8:30 A.M., *50-minutes ahead* of schedule, to "water" its cars, thirsty after the draining that the laving and shaving executives had given them in grooming for the day ahead. Beside the quenching, car-men gave the red hot running gear a going-over and saw to it that everything was ready for the faster-than-ordinary running on ahead.

Fearful of taking even its allotted ten-minutes, *Super-2* charged away from the water "plugs," showed her "tail feathers" to the gang at the depot, and chased her blaring air-horn out of Winslow town.

Along the up-grade east of Winslow, *Super-2's* trio of Diesels dug into the rails and took the 385-tons of cars climbing 1,649 feet at 75 m.p.h. and pulled into Gallup at 10:26 A.M., paring 10¼ minutes off the regular schedule in just that 127.7 miles and a minute less than one hour from the 14 hours-25 minutes carded for the 728 miles from Los Angeles!

Pausing just long enough to take on a fresh engine crew and allow the city-folk passengers to have a peek at bands of Indians gathered below their stateroom windows, *Super-2* was again impatiently on her way, moving away fast enough to ruffle a number of Indian blankets as *Navajo's* rounded tail sped past the end of the station-platform.

⎯⎯Super Chief⎯⎯

Between Belen and Isleta, *Super-2* ran into one of those typical New Mexico Maytime, heaven-opening rain squalls and rode it all the way into Albuquerque. The arrival was smack in the midst of the executives' lunch, 12:47 P.M., and the cars were drenched, but still *1 hour-14 minutes ahead* of the timecard.

For more years than any of us cares to recall, Santa Fe advertising pictured its trains at the Albuquerque depot with a chiaroscuro of Santo Dominguez Indians offering their hand-fashioned blankets, basketry, jewelry, or other souvenir impedimentia to people off the cars. In most instances, sunny, blue-skied instances, the delineation squared, but not there in that torrential downpour on an all-out dash of *Super-2*. As a matter of fact, they didn't even bother to open the train doors except the one that the conductor barged out of to slosh down the steps and into the waiting room, his yellow slicker flaring out behind him in a sudden gust of wind.

The "execs," thoughtful and reflective in the thunder and lightning, snug at their damask-napered perches, went right on eating, relieved at not having to set feet in the *déluge*.

Rain, especially that heavy rain, competed harshly with sound inside the tube that was *Super-2* and, sensing the pluvial interdiction, the "execs' " table-talk all but ceased, and the cozy diner, hushed, rolled wetly past the gray-walled depot and out into the downpour to make its way under an ugly sky brimming with dirty gray clouds.

East of Albuquerque, Santa Fe rail truly begins clambering onto the spine of The Rockies, threading its way up out of the red earth and along trackage torn out of unyielding, there-since-time-began, bouldered battlements of awesome, unfathomable scale.

Beyond Lamy, *Super-2* barged into 7,400-foot Glorieta Pass and rambled through the mossy, wet-walled slashes that formed the ominous-sounding Apache Canyon. Throttling down, the Diesel threesome fumed out plumes of nearly black exhaust and serpentined their carloads of junketing businessmen ever upward. Ribera, Chapelle, Romero———tiny, altitude-bound way stations———slid by the glossy armor of *The Super* as she bent her way around a ribboning of curves and into Las Vegas at 3:32 P.M., *an hour and twenty-one minutes ahead* of the advertised time.

In front of the 'dobe colored Spanish-style depot, setting on a cart spotted close to where *Cochiti's* kitchen door would pull up, were two bushel baskets filled with ice, watched over by a lean man with a weathered face smoking a dirty, well-caked briar. No sooner had the diner's wheels stopped than steward Peter Tausch was down the three ladder-rungs, headed for those baskets. Digging into the cracked ice, he pulled out two fat, shimmering, caught-that-morning mountain trout.

Hefting them from hand to hand with narrow-eyed *expertise*,

151

Tausch sniffed each trout, dug out a half-dozen more, gently prodded their fleshy middles and then, since the two-minute stop was already half over, perfunctorily divied up the contents of both baskets into one, which the pipe-smoking angler lifted through the kitchen door just as Tausch's backside disappeared around the corner and the brakes released.

Two short snorts of the air horn and *Super-2* was gone. The few passengers who witnessed the trout transaction were secure in the knowledge that the finny beauties would soon fill the diner's passageway with the camp-fire fragrance of their grilling over a bed of Mesquite charcoal in Eddie Dyke's glowing broiler. M-m-m-m-m.

While the "execs" langored away the cocktail hour, it was then getting on toward four-thirty, ... they set *Acoma* to humming with equal parts of admiring rhetoric on the Prima Vera panelling and who knew whom on the Coast. Out in the pelting rain, *Super-2's* power-bank wound its way, growling and grating, up the 3.3 percent grade through Wagon Mound, Springer, Hebron, and into Raton for three minutes to change crews and pick up a 2-10-2 steam "helper" engine.

They were still way ahead of the booked time, actually *92-minutes*, and pushing aside minutes at a bullying clip.

Steamer No. 925 coupled on ahead of "2's" crimson nose, like an old exercise boy escorting a thoroughbred to the starting gate, and off the *four* locomotives went ... snarling, smoking, puffing, and raising holy hell in the rain-soaked valley approach to the thousand feet they'd have to climb in just under eight miles.

The "elevator ride" up the 7,622 feet to Raton Tunnel, apex of the system, stretched, full length, every sinew of horsepower at the head of *Super-2* as they penetrated the black bore, breathing hard and dripping. Geared into a coaster "run," they headed down the descending half of the tunnel and burst out of the half-mile maw and into Colorado, where rain still dogged the flyer.

The push-off from Raton Tunnel was reminiscent of a young-ster on an old Flexible Flyer sled, feet up in the "steering" handles and rope held tight for a fast ride. *Super-2* began its flight down the 1,630 feet of "hill" to Trinidad, fifteen miles away, much like the sleigh rider, bound and determined to slash price-less seconds off the running time.

Second call to dinner found *Super-2* in the midst of her down-hill run, and "execs" who were caught in that slaloming between their staterooms and *Cochiti* could have used ski poles. Pin-wheels of sparks from the steady-working brake shoes sent sprays of orange bits of steel up past the diner's long windows, to be eerily magnified and kaleidoscoped by the rain drops covering those windows . . . the pyrotechnic display, coupled with the pell-mell speed, elicited sedate "oohs" and equally genteel "ahhs."

The hissing-hot mountain trout, branded darkly by the broiler interstices, nuzzled among puffs of parsley and pimento-draped lemon wedges to also elicit salivating praises and signal the triumph of the gustatory over the mechanical. Only the sharp gravity of *Super-2's* get-in-and-get-out stopping for La Junta interrupted the enthusiastic dinner chatter————that and the good-sized after-supper crowd gathered there on the wet platform to welcome the Special. The several hundred mountain folk, waving vigorously in front of the three-story depot and congregating directly below their tables, did divert the "execs" from the panorama of Tauschian delicacies, but not for long and not until they waved back with studied forebearance.

The rain was slackening and one could see by the depot clock that it was 7:37 P.M., *one hour and thirty-eight minutes before* it was scheduled to arrive————faster than any train would ever sweep across the 1,236 miles from Los Angeles! All in all, the "good will" run was setting a blistering pace and, happily for Santa Fe, maintaining it.

Relieving engineer Tucker Taylor, raincoated and grip in hand, was standing trackside when *Super-2* splashed into La Junta but, instead of mounting to the cab of the red-snouted lead Diesel, he first walked quickly back to the side of the third unit, two-year-old, long-in-harness "512," idling almost serenely and looking as though it had done all this before which, of course, it had. However, that night "512" and its two E 1A *matelots* would generate power and achieve speeds foreign even to the wise-in-the-way-of-the-road demonstration Diesel.

Perhaps because he knew what lay ahead, Taylor ran his hand over the aluminum-painted flanks of ol' "512," somewhat like a stage driver patting the foreleg of his lead horse. One *had* to relate to reciprocating old lions such as "512;" they had personality, and in an agreeably structural way————a line here, an appendage there————transcended the purely mechanical.

Having made peace with his grizzled third power unit, "Tuck" Taylor hurried forward, took to the cab of No. 2, and settled into his armchair for the 202.4 miles of gently descending gradient into Dodge City, a bee line of right-of-way known as "the racetrack."

Taylor snapped off the customary pair of warning burps on the air-horn and gave *Super-2* the downbeat that sent her on her way under a plume of full-rich Diesel fumery. Charging past the Strain Ice House and rattling the pen fences of the stockyard, the flyer was out of town and gone.

— Super Chief

Slumping into a deep armchair in *Navajo's* snug lounge, musician-attorney John Raskin lighted a cigar and opened a copy of the La Junta *Tribune-Democrat*, interrupting his scanning to glance idly out the tan-draped window at a townscape already darting by pretty fast. The wheel flanges bit hard into the rails and their inordinate clanging triggered an auditory alert in Raskin, riveting his attention on the fast-fading twin strips of gleaming rail disappearing by the minute, faster and faster, from under the lamp-lighted ebony end table.

Two of Raskin's fellow lounge occupants sensed his awareness, and it wasn't long 'til all three were up on the arms of their chairs, eyes glued to the wildly animating scenery transitorily visible outside the curved proscenium of *Navajo's* glass-enclosed *galleria*. Pretty soon, other "execs," alerted by the punching sidesway and mounting wheel noises, found their way into the observation car and, guided by porter Joe Chapman to "ringside" seats in the lounge, pressed their faces to any window that was handy.

Nineteen miles out of La Junta, *Super-2*, in full cry, zoomed by Las Animas and treated the watchers in *Navajo* to a split-second echo-blast that the tiny depot hurled back at *Super-2*. One "exec," wise in the ways of train riding, said, "Let's, for th' hell of it, see just how fast this thing is goin'."

Pulling out a silver pocket watch, he stared at it and out the window for a nonce, and then intoned abruptly, "Thirty-two seconds, 'bout 113 miles 'n hour!" *That* livened up the lounge alright, and dazzled the dozen or so sharing the ride in the rocketing observation end. Of course, what was nearly as impressive as the miles-per-hour announcement was the fact that that watch-holder was at all able to spot——in the dark——two mileposts going at that blurring speed. You see, the elapsed time between mileposts was what gave him *The Super's* 113 m.p.h.

pace.

A little further on, he wouldn't need mileposts. All he or any of the "execs" would have to do was watch for two stations. Ordinarily carded over the 10.8 miles from Caddoa to Prowers, Colorado in six-minutes, that night the three Diesels took *Super-2* plummeting past Prowers in just five-and-a-half minutes, an *average* of 117.6 m.p.h.! The very sound of those 5,400 horsepower bearing down on him sent the agent at Prowers fleeing into the depot where, from behind the safety of his bay-window desk, he waved an "All clear" to *The Super's* brakeman, also behind glass at the rear door of *Navajo.* At 117 m.p.h., one didn't open train doors!

Quite a few of the businessmen———at-table while *Super-2* was romping at three figures———savored more than their succulent *à brun* mountain trout. They exulted in their landed flight in the "hundreds" and even shouted as the flyer, air-horn screaming, blew by Lamar, Granada, and Amity. Since 1901, Santa Fe Limiteds had come charging down the hill from La Junta, but never had any of them done it relishing the sprint as was "Tuck" Taylor as he laid the whip to his lathered Diesel charges that drizzly mid-May evening in 1937.

Super-2, preview running out of Los Angeles, kept right on spinning off the miles, setting up a fearful din every time she went through a town or station. Preceded by the relentless bellowing of an air-horn that pervaded everything for a mile around, the glistening flyer———given its head———seemed bent on blotting out any performance that a Santa Fe train had ever made. She was intent upon scratching her name in any and every record book being kept there in the mid-Thirties (forty-some years later, her performance that night would still stand unchallenged).

In her race for all the marbles, *Super-2*, as though out of a giant catapult, shot across the Kansas border, thundered by Coolidge doing 109 m.p.h., "pinched" down to "90" for Syracuse, aired-off, and swept the next 51½ miles under her wheels in a shade over thirty-four minutes!

Throttling out deftly, Taylor, his eyes darting from track to railroad watch, sent *Super-2* off-and-running again, obliterating the miles, and after rattling windows on the east end of Garden City, blew in and out of Pierceville, 12.3 miles down the line, in seven-and-a-half minutes———a fraction under "100."

Super-2 glides through Streator, Illinois, on the morning of June 20, 1937, en route to Chicago. — L. E. GRIFFITH

Not long after the *Super* cleared town, the second section of the *Chief* pulls into Streator with *Super-1's* old diesel locomotives on the head end. The second unit is the "512," a diesel demonstrator belonging to General Motors. — L. E. GRIFFITH

With her cargo of "execs" still in a dither, albeit a staid one, over their bomb-run ride——happily imbibing and trying to navigate the lounges and rocking corridors——"Tuck" Taylor aimed his gleaming, rain-dappled train down the eastbound "main" of the mud-colored, hip-roofed Dodge City Depot. It was 10:01 P.M.——just 139-minutes after leaving La Junta, 202 miles back. Taylor had run the "racetrack" at an average of almost "90" and brought *Super-2* into Dodge *an hour-and-fifty-four minutes ahead* of the regular schedule. Beside the long-distance time-cut, they chipped away 16 minutes from the allotted timing just in those last 202 miles, *averaging* 87.2 m.p.h.!

A misty rain persisted and dripped from the second story eaves of the old station building. Puddles along the weathered brick platform reflected all the lights that had been left on to welcome *The Super* on its fourth and last preview run in the two-week series (May 3–17). A crowd milled about the platform. The train-watchers wouldn't have much time to indulge their passion and they knew it. Hurrying from car to car, they strained their necks for glimpses into the elegant cars, ogling as best they could the warmly lighted panelling and draperies and, in some cases, the snug, snowy white Pullman berths made up for the night. Youngsters, up way past their bedtimes, were hoisted on shoulders and, with that six-foot height advantage, their little faces came nearly level with those of the "execs" who bothered to stare back.

The car men——squatting and leaning underneath the perspiring Pullmans——weren't exactly pleased with the curious getting in the way when they had only three minutes to do their inspecting, but said nothing because it wasn't every day *Super-2* loped into their prairie town in the midst of setting a record. Engineers got off and on, water was pumped aboard the Diesels for the steam generators, a few sacks of charcoal were hauled up into the diner, two short snorts of the air-horn "called in" the rear brakeman, the bell-ringer went on, and *Super-2*——in just the length of its cars——was rolling quickly ... flashing its purple sign and red markers as it bade "Goodnight" to the faithful standing there in the rain to wave "Farewell."

Crimson-nosed *Super Chief*, with 2A and 2B on the head-end, streaks through Chillicothe, Illinois, on August 29, 1937. Everything is running smoothly and the diesel maintainer is enjoying the scenery from his open window in 2B. — R. V. MEHLENBECK

13

The change to Central Time made it 11:04 P.M., May 16th, 1937, when *Super-2* took off out of Dodge City, bed time for most of the executives, many of whom had been up since early morning. Only a few diehards in *Acoma*—one dozing under *The Journal*, two sipping *Courvoisier* brandy, and four playing cribbage—spurned the siren song of Old Morpheus and kept barman Al Day at his post. Washing glasses and keeping a weather eye on the wall clock, Day busied himself in the lavendar glow from red and blue bulbs burning in two plastic-covered niches bordering the inlaid Kachina back-bar. Dance tunes with a muted-trumpet lead flowed out of the bar-front radio.

A sudden, firm shot of brake pressure crossing Manchon Street telegraphed the "running air test" which brakeman Seth Weller acknowledged, "pin wheeling" his lantern out the vestibule door of *Navajo*. Brakes valved off and *Super-2* lunged forward, immediately gathering momentum. Weller slammed the upper half of the vestibule door into its big catch and stepped to his right into the hushed air of *Taos*, where the stateroom doors—some open, some ajar—offered a diorama of the bedding-down ritual in all its varied aspects. *Oraibi*, likewise quieting for the night, presented much the same sights and sounds—all of them to the accompaniment of muffled wheel-clicking that seeped, barely discernible, through the cork-and-carpeted floor.

Exquisite Interiors had the following to say about lounge car *Acoma*. "Centering attention in the cocktail lounge is a splendid inlay in the panel behind the bar. It represents a Kachina, a ceremonial dancer of one of the Southwest Indian tribes. Taking the part of a leifite ancestor, he is wearing a mouth-mask and holds in one hand a conventionalized ear of corn, in the other a dance stave. Over him is a rainbow, with a cloud at either end, and at each side, the symbol of a mountain. The consummate skill of design is matched by the perfect choice of words for the inlay."

By then the *Super-2* Diesels really had their shoulders into the load and were, as the old saying used to go, "headed for the barn" which, in that instance, happened to be Newton, 153.1 miles down the line. By the time the flyer flamed through Ellinwood, doing better than "100," it was 12:04 A.M. and the windows of its staterooms were all dark, or at least showed just a blue night light here and there. Only when the observation end flew by a station could a bystander see the lone light on in the string of rain-coated windows—the silver-and-turquoise lamp burning in the very last window of *Navajo*, an incandescent valedictory to any and all who watched her go by.

In precisely 50 minutes, *Super-2's* load of slumbering "execs"—secured in their stainless pauldronry—had hurtled through the Kansas blackness to wipe away the 74.3 miles into Newton at an *average* of 89.1 m.p.h.! Sliding into the trim depot like a baserunner, it seemed as though the wheels still hadn't touched ground. They were into Newton *two hours and six minutes before* the timetable decreed they should be and carmen and switchmen yelled their approval as they clustered around the wet-faced cars that brushed by them for entry.

The moment the hot, oily-smelling wheels crunched to a stop, two switchmen darted between the hind unit of the Diesels and the baggage car and, ever so gently, uncoupled the power units from the train. They drifted forward, just past a switch, for more uncoupling.

From the cab of the last of the three Diesels, old "512," hostler Clay Ziegler shoved his head and shoulders out the side window and, with no more cylinder-commotion than if he had cleared his throat, slipped "512" over onto the adjoining track and then, barely audible, mumbling along toward the roundhouse.

With "512" in-the-clear, the two E 1A's, the shiny "new" ones, were shunted back to the cars and again, with a feather touch, coupled on to *Super-2*. Clumping off in the middle distance, "512" had done its work: lent its stodgy bulk to the unblooded but esthetically more appealing E 1A units, helping pull the eager-to-fly *Super* over a lot of rugged terrain quicker than any Santa Fe train would ever do it.

Small wonder, then, that hostler Ziegler grinned knowingly as he throttled "512" along in the darkness. Looking back at the crimson noses of the Diesels that would take *Super-2* the rest of the way into Chicago, "512" seemed to him somewhat reminiscent of the much-practiced "JV" fullback who fights his way down to the ten-yard line only to watch a sophomore halfback go in to score.

As was typical of an all-sleeper train in the wee hours of the morning, only a handful of the "execs" lifted their window shades for a peek at where they were; otherwise, the little railroad town would remain forever a mystery to the bulk of Santa Fe's guests. Another mystery of sorts, at least to those who slept through Newton, would be how three Diesels took *Super-2* out of Los Angeles and only two finished the trip.

Coupling, switching, servicing, and crew-changing dispensed with, the omnipresent brakeman's lantern waved *Super-2* out of Newton and on its way to the place where, so the song said, "everything was up to date": Kansas City. When *Navajo's* markerlights whipped past the depot door, the waiting room clock read "1:02."

A sudden pulseless hush pressed against his eardrums and awakened Aaron Marcus, causing the graying executive to lift one of the tiny shades of his twin upper-berth windows and look out on a deserted platform and up at the underside of the concourse level of Kansas City's Union Station. Under the blue night-light, his gold watch—inscribed "from the Pasadena Chamber of Commerce"—read "3:30." Satisfied and oriented, Marcus lowered the shade, snapped off the light, and went back to sleep.

It is worth noting, though, that *Super-2* had just run the 185.1 miles from Newton in 148 minutes to average a respectable 75 m.p.h. and put the cars down at "KC" *two hours-thirty minutes ahead* of time! The record pace was still intact with only 451 miles to go.

There was a good deal of activity up at the head end—five figures climbed the side ladders and, arranging three camp stools, took their seats in Diesel "2's" cab. New Engineer Frank Petska slid into his cushioned spot on the right side; Fireman Liam Flaherty eased into the left chair; road foreman of engines for the Missouri Division, Jim Campbell, pulled his stool right alongside Petska so they could work like coxswain and stroke; Air Brake Supervisor Art Reeves took his place beside Flaherty; mechanical Superintendent Joe McGoff leaned his stool against the back wall of the cab.

It was an odd-looking assembly—Petska and Flaherty in coveralls and the three "brass" wearing business suits and fedora hats. That run of *The Super Chief* was damned important and not to be slighted by the powers of the Motive Power Department.

Since there was no station "work" to be done on that good-will run at Kansas City, slim six-footer Petska throttled his Diesels to life at 3:36 A.M. and with them, led the way out of the "trough" with quiet assurance, while behind him the Pullmans glided sinuously through the switches and into the "Main." Petska, with an eye for everything, handled the train as if it were his own and, that morning, was demonstrating his virtuosity even more prominently than usual.

—*Super Chief*

Under the wiry Petska's skilled hands, it wasn't but a few hundred yards 'til *Super-2* resumed its no-nonsense attack on time and miles and the accelerating Diesels bounced their blattering exhaust off the concrete "sounding board" that walled in the curving, sunken trackage they were riding out of "Kaycee." The twin skeins of steel rail unravelled—faster and faster—under the devouring pilot . . . "40"-"50"-/"60"-"70" . . . and, when they spun through the outskirts of Sheffield, registered "75" on the dual speedometers. They cleared Sugar Creek with one leap and sped into Cement City.

Precisionist Petska slipped his watch out of a coverall breast pocket with monotonous frequency, cradling it between his first and little fingers (never in his palm), thumb extended, right angle to the first finger—semaphore fashion. "The Watch," sacred to any and all train operation, caused Petska to notch-out to the next "run" and set *Super-2* sailing ever faster.

Henrietta, Hardin, and Norborne were sensed simply as shrieks from the horn and momentary blurs of buildings streaked with light, buildings that blanched under the blasts of warning hurled at them. The Diesels' wheels skimmed the track with a high-pitched "wheeeee" . . . something like sled runners on ice. At Carrollton, which they seared with a shattering roar, a big yellow tomcat—probably the station mascot—fled beneath the depot for sanctuary of any sort. At the end of *Navajo*, the purple medallion glowed through the night to greet the world as they passed.

Petska romped *Super-2* along the hypnotizing, headlighted trail for the twenty-nine miles to Rothville where, at 5:07, they

163

thundered by just as the first light of day silhouetted the horizon-line in the eastern distance. Seven miles down the way, dawn sifting softly over the landscape, he slowed for the Yard Limit at Marceline. Slipping switches, squealing flanges, and disappearing across Laurel Street, *Super-2* would, in the next 112 miles, be confronted by a line with more kinks in it than last summer's garden hose. Between the throttle, horn cord, and the brake valve, the canny Petska kept as busy as a kitten on a marble floor. The cab was alive with the sigh-and-cry of compressed air which orchestrated his virtuoso brake-valving in the battle for every foot of every curve, a fight which, in most cases, he won.

On east they sped under an awakening magenta sky. Robins, mobilized for flight, rose in startled clouds as they passed and, a few yards further on, they flushed other wings out of moist, grassy havens. The speedometers showed "85," about where Petska liked to keep them on straight stretches to make the 216.5 miles in about 200 minutes. *Super-2* swayed and lunged into an endless variety of Missouri curvatures, charging up to the beginning of tangents, dragging its "feet" through the arcing rail, and then racing out the opening end into the straightaways.

It was about 6:50 on Petska's Hamilton as *Super-2* curved into Bricker, sighted the Mississippi, and headed up river. Minutes later, he throttled down the fuming E 1A's, rushed by the brick shop-buildings, waved to the yardmaster just emerging from the "reading room," and cushioned to a stop beside the service "plugs" at Shopton just as his watch ticked to 6:57. They had made it from "KC" in 200 minutes and averaged "65" in the bargain. "Well, not bad, but it coulda been better," Petska exhaled to the ruddy face and gray sideburns that preceded six feet-205 pounds of John Martin into the left side door of the cab. The stolid "new" engineer tossed his bag on the floor and allowed as how this was "some damned run," eliciting a sharp nod from the slender Petska already retreating down the fireman's side. Shouting "Good luck" up to Martin, Petska added, "Keep an eye on that steam boiler; 's been acting up ever since 'Dodge'."

Alone, Martin raised the leather chair a notch or two and settled heavily into his perch. The early morning sun cut through the windshield and called for setting and adjusting the visor. Fireman Walt Carley brusquely shouldered his way through the door from the engine room, grumbling darkly about the "damned steamboiler" . . . spitting the overflow from a lipful of

164

In the locomotive cab, Engineer Frank Templeton, hand on the throttle, attends to his job. Back in the cars, passengers are in the diner, or having drinks in the lounge.

"Copenhagen" snuff out the open door at which he stationed himself. Mock cheers from the yard crews accompanied the loud peal of the "Highball" at Martin's right ear.

7:02 ... and *Super-2* slipped past the yard office, the ice house, and "reefer" platform. Martin throttled out just enough to get up revolutions for the mile-and-a-half roll into Ft. Madison. At the Fort, *Super-2* turned northeast and then curved sharply right and started south across the long double-track drawbridge over the Mississippi coming off at East Ft. Madison. Done with the slow-order for the bridge, Martin opened the throttle a notch, the pitch of the hum beyond the steel bulkhead at his back rose a fraction of a tone, and *Super-2* glided out of the bridge approach and on to the sun-drenched main line.

His left hand worked the throttle; his right was "free" to manage air-horn, bell, brake valve, signal to the rear, or whatever else.

165

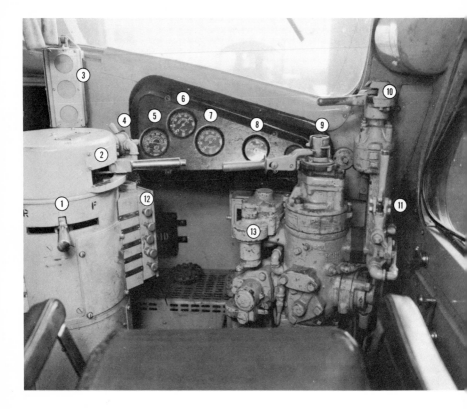

Engineer's Control Station of Electro-Motive Diesel-electric locomotive No. 2.

1. Reverse Lever
2. Throttle Lever (1-8 positions)
3. Automatic Train Control Cab Signal
4. Locomotive Bell Valve
5. Equalizing Reservoir and Main Reservoir Air Gauge
6. Brake Pipe and Brake Cylinder Air Gauge
7. Application Pipe and Supression Air Gauge
8. Speedometer
9. Independent Brake Valve
10. Automatic Brake Valve
11. Sander Valve
12. Switches for Control Generator Field Fuel Pump, Attendant
    Call, and Defroster
13. Feed Valve
14. Light Switches, Headlight Bright, Headlight Dim, Train
    Number Lights, Gauge Lights, and Classification Lights

166

15. Speed Recorder
16. Hot Water Heater Valve
17. Hot Water Heater Valve
18. Window Wiper Switch
19. Pneumatic Windshield Wiper Mechanism
20. Whistle Cords, one for Horn Facing Forward, the Other for Horn Facing Toward Train

He kept his right foot glued to the pedal of the "Dead Man's Control," which was set for instant automatic action in case of emergency—so long as the brake handle was in place. In the throttle (Controller), by the way, were eight notches, each of which was translated into a change of 75 r.p.m. or 120 horsepower. The Master Control operated in *series* up to thirty miles an hour, in *parallel* from "thirty" to "sixty," and in *shunt* above "Sixty."

It could happen only in Chicago! The *Super Chief* of the Santa Fe Railway and the *Dixie Flagler* of the Chicago & Eastern Illinois Railroad were the nation's only streamliners from opposite coasts to meet in the same station. The *Super Chief* had just arrived from its 39-hour journey from Los Angeles, while the *Dixie Flagler* was about to depart Dearborn Station for the coast of Florida. — TRAINS MAGAZINE

Gradually, Martin's power duo gathered speed; *Super-2* raised its voice and the throttle handle was brought back, notch after notch. The song of the machinery rose from mezzo to contralto as the stocky Martin's big hand on the horn-cord sent out a warning that could be heard for miles, heard but unfamiliar at that hour to farmers in their fields, farmers not aware that *The Super Chief* was running more than two-and-a-half hours *ahead* of time! Between Dallas City and Lomax, Martin had his 3,600 "horses" at full gallop. Ahead unrolled a perfect path of steel, which *Super-2* was treading with such poise that anyone in the cab was unaware of the velocity save for the scud of roadside scenery.

From inside that cab, minus noise, minus heat, minus dust, with supreme *hauteur*, they annihilated mile after mile. Barefooted boys, dawdling toward school, hopped up on rail fences along the right-of-way to marvel as *The Super* scorched by, in some instances stamping its awesome signet on pennies or horseshoe nails that they had placed on the tracks. With a condescending hip-fake of its observation end, *Super-2's* purple sign and glowing markers threw back their images at the wide-eyed youngsters and, in seconds, were lost to them in a swirling cloud of dust.

Chef Carlos Gardini hangs onto the broiler bar while the pitching *Super Chief* kitchen careens through a sharp curve. Here marbled sirloins were grilled to perfection at 90 miles-per-hour.

14

About 7:30 A.M., May 17th, 1937, speeding along, well into Illinois—on the outskirts of Stronghurst (208.9 miles west of Chicago), almost everyone of the "execs" were up and stirring, and the cars reverberated with pre-breakfast throat-clearing, nose-blowing, lotion-slapping, and apertural noise-making.

Congregating in the aisles wasn't easy considering the pell-mell pace that *Super-2* was setting, so the majority of the "execs" remained seated while they waited for breakfast. Even veteran porters were having trouble keeping their balance while they stripped the berths of early risers.

Engineer Martin was treating the "execs" to a go-for-broke ride and blurring the western Illinois countryside as he went about his work ... notched in "Run 2." Steward Peter Tausch, acutely aware of the speeds that *Super-2* was making, advanced the morning meal a half-hour and sent waiter "Wixie" Wilson lurching through the rocketing cars—chimes in hand—to announce, "Fuhst c-a-w-l t' brayuk-fust."

Cochiti's stoves and broilers were hot and ready for the first thirty-six "execs" who teetered—gravity buffeted—into its sunshiny expanse and sat down, gingerly and gratefully, as the car slammed into another curve. Tausch wanted his guests to go away with warm memories of *Super-2* and their once-in-a-life-time trip so, on that last-morning-out, he spared nothing from his burgeoning larder ... a treasure trove of the finest in railway dining, *Super Chief* dining.

The bright cadmium of frosty glasses of orange juice speckled the snowy tablecloths. Figs the size of golf-balls thrust their plump, glossy faces up out of dishes of cream as thick as yoghurt. Great slabs of rosey ham, broiler-seared and bubbling, sat like pink sculpture beside done-to-a-turn, golden hot cakes that framed enormous butter-coated eggs with gleaming yolks—all of it accented with cakey cubes of ochre-and-brown country fried potatoes. Pure maple syrup put a coating on the griddle cakes as deep and as lustrous as the face of a Stradivarius.

One table groaned beneath four orders of piping-hot, paper-thin chipped beef, smothered in creamy gravy and piled in mountains over rafts of crisp toast!

Center car, President Bledsoe and his three guests chose to roam the embossed menu: shirred eggs, white as alabaster and lassoed in strips of lean bacon, rode in an emerald periphery of parsley; succulent filets of calf liver—*sautéed* to a buttery, earthy brown—nestled under straps of crinkly, sizzling bacon; charcoal-smudged lamp chops—bearing the black diamond scorings from turnings on the broiler—posed in a leafy surf of watercress; ebony-dappled puffs of raisin bread French toast—baked high and pebbly-brown—floated over a platter slathered with table-spooned dollops of orange marmalade.

The grainy perfumery of bran and corn muffins, cracked open steamily, tantalized the nostrils. And over it all wafted the aroma of rich, black coffee rising smokily out of Ms. Coulter's *primitif* cups.

No doubt about it, Peter Tausch and his chefs, Gardini and Dyke, took that last *Super-2* "Ballyhoo" breakfast to Elysian heights, offering fabled fare that many of the "execs" enthused about for years after they were back in California and *The Super Chief* was but a shiny 'though somewhat misted memory.

Churning along at "85"—well into the "home stretch"—about four miles east of Stronghurst ... B-O-N-G! ... the Pyrometer alarm split the droning warmth of the cab!

"Damn," Martin rasped as he throttled down instinctively and at the same instant saw, in the side mirror, smoke and sparks spewing out the exhaust stack.

Eyeing the drop in oil pressure and the flashing red lens, Jim Campbell growled, kicked over his stool, and bolted for the door.

" 's a damned blown piston, sure as hell," he shot over his shoulder as he disappeared into the engine room, McGoff and Reeves right on his heels. Four strides and they were beside the yammering engines, balancing themselves in the pitching gangway alongside maintainers Tom Blickle and Frank Golden, all sniffing suddenly at the smoking "cap" of cylinder No. 4 in the aft engine.

In what seemed a single motion, Blickle swiped at the switch with an oily glove, shut down the godawful clangoring Winton engine, and ripped at the lift-screw on the "cap." Uncapped, No. 4 was a wipe-out, *scored piston head and cylinder liner!*

Obviously, No. 4 had succumbed to the rigors of 2000-plus miles of sustained wide-open running and fallen prey to the always lurking percentages of internal combustion cantankerousness—a not uncommon occurrence with those earliest underpowered, unpredictable Diesels.

Reasoning that they were only about three hours out of Chicago and going for a record, Blickle and Golden and the trio of "brass" opted to have the blown piston repaired at the end of the line. After all, one cylinder out of forty-eight wouldn't have any appreciable effect on their speed-making capabilities; it was just those minutes they'd lost, slowing to assess the scope of the damage, that irked them so.

So, while Martin cruised along at "50," Blickle and Golden hurriedly cut-out the faulty cylinder, blocked the water "ports," re-ignited the sound cylinders, and waved "Go ahead" to Campbell, who already had the bulk-head door open so he could signal Martin to get moving again.

Given the "go ahead," the bulky engineer throttled out in seconds, angered that, in the slow-down, precious minutes had eluded him on the tag end of the most notable run he'd ever have the chance to make.

With "4" buttoned up and Martin rolling along in "high run" again, Campbell and Reeves set up their camp stools and resumed their vigils in the cab. McGoff, on the other hand, remained with Blickle and Golden and kept a weather eye on a couple of other potential trouble spots brought on by the day-

With dust flying across the right-of-way, the *Super Chief* roars past the farming center of Edelstein, Illinois, on August 29, 1937. — R. V. MEHLENBECK

and-a-half of bang-up, full-bore running.

At Galesburg, Jim Campbell relieved Martin. The "Dead Man's Control" had to be handled gingerly as they shifted pressure, like two boys trying to weigh on the same scale for only one penny. Campbell warmed to his work with a sharp touch on the throttle and brake valve and cannonaded the grimy E 1A's through the race-course straightaway from Princeville to Edelstein, swooping down Nine Mile Hill and into a "slow" through Chillicothe.

The hawk-eyed road foreman raced *Super-2* along relentlessly, fighting grimly to recover any and all seconds he could after the piston episode. Grade crossings came and went like yard-markers on a football field, and rock ballast and dirt were suctioned up to form a clinging cloud at the wheels like a misty dust ruffle on a long four-poster.

Crossing chimes rang out, or at least so it seemed, as closely as church bells, and automobiles at the crossings kept further back than they ever had—alerted by the almost beseeching, bleating tremolo of the air horn atop *Super-2's* Diesels.

Sensing the nearness of the home depot, *Super-2* lunged against Campbell's braking "leash"—at "100," the wheels turning so fast that they set off a constant stream of sparks between those wheels and the rails . . . a veritable Roman candle display when the brake shoes bit home!

Bustling in to the tree-lined pastoralism of Streator, Campbell pulled up for an irksome momentary stop at a crossing. Watches came out like rain clouds and anxious feet tapped off every second of that "damnable" stop, as Martin put it.

"CLEAR BOARD" and Campbell's hand blurred as he released the brakes! *Super-2* jumped ahead like a running guard, plowing up turf and sending back the disdainful gaze of her rear markers until she swerved through the east end of town and was lost to view.

The 52 miles to Joliet were an indistinguishable jumble of fields, farm fences, and frame depots ricocheting their earth-brown facades off the gleaming sides of the fast-flying *Super*. Each time they passed a "cut" of freight cars on a siding, it sounded like instant full-gain on a giant stereo. "Praise be" for the sound insulation that Budd had packed into *Super-2's* walls!

Super CHIEF

Alerted by telegraph from Millsdale, the Santa Fe agent at Joliet announced officiously that *The Super Chief* was on its way!

Clamping a blue agent's cap squarely on his close-cropped head, he led a doughty band of after-breakfast faithful out of the gray limestone depot and on to the brick platform. Way off in the distance, the sharp-eyed among them detected a pinpoint of yellow light and a radiating heat cloud looming out of the west that was the hurrying *Super.*

Good-natured laughter pealed through the few dozen and the omnipresent "expert" among them—there's always *one* "expert"—held forth on all sorts of railway information . . . most of it wrong.

The headlight beam grew bigger and brighter by the second. The more daring of the group edged closer to the track, warned back by the patriarchal, all-knowing agent.

By then the ground rumbled and the rails "sang" from *The Super's* quickening steel-wheeled advance and, before they all knew it . . . WHOOSH!, all in one BIG, metallic UP-CLOSE panorama, the glowering headlamp, dirt-crusted/bug-spattered crimson nose, clanging bell, hot oil smells, smoking brakes, and little, grainy billows from the sander jarred past the upturned faces . . . slowing just enough to clump, machine gun-like, over crossovers, crossings, and other incidents of passage, including the Rock Island main line at the end of the station.

Yes, all that they had come to see was by them in a rush—only the purple herald, scurrying toward Chicago, looked back fleetingly at them, grateful for their encouragement *en passant.*

—*Super* CHIEF

Just outside Joliet, Campbell and Martin again exchanged places . . . and wry grins.

" 's all yours, John. *You* take 'er in and get the attention," the road foreman jibed as he slid away from the right-hand window and down into the "well" between engineer and fireman.

When Martin wrapped his thick fingers around the throttle, there were just 37 miles left to go and his watch read "10:15."

In short order, he took his racing E 1A's vaulting across the iridescent Des Plaines and conquered Lockport doing "75." The town of Romeo was gone in a flash, and the Diesels' exhaust bounced mutedly off the grassy embankments near Lemont.

Looking down from those "cuts" in the earth, one might have

176

seen luggage stacked neatly—at-the-ready—in the car vestibules. By Willow Springs, porters were putting on their own Pullman-badged caps and getting the "execs' " fedoras and straws out of tan paper bags, to be brushed off with lingering theatrics. Whisk brooms were everywhere! The staterooms tingled with last-minute bustle and friendly pre-detraining *badinage*.

Sitting in deserted *Cochiti* at a sun-drenched, clothless table, steward Tausch jotted down the last notes on a Fred Harvey report-sheet and fiddled nervously with the knot of his yellow linen necktie. Chicago nearly always offered bright biological "prospects" to the dapper Teuton, and that trip was to be no exception. Around the ruminating Tausch, the dining car men chortled and jostled one another in the cramped, linen-littered aisles, eager to be getting home.

Dressing "to the nines" also went on in the crew-quarters of *Acoma*, the men primping and preparing for their 33½-hour layover in the "Windy City," good ol' "Chi."

Back in *Navajo*, porter Chapman hummed softly as he stripped the last of the two drawing rooms' berths and stuffed soiled linen in big canvas laundry bags.

A lovely aura of aquamarine bathed *Navajo's* observation lounge, color created by the sun glinting off the top of a bookcase and reflecting up on the turquoise ceiling. Three "execs" soaked-up the morning sun there, smoking fine cigars and reveling in the last few miles of emerald-and-amber Illinois.

McCook... Nerska... Corwith... and *voilà*, the sharp-shadowed Chicago skyline stood high ahead as *Super-2* eased by the 12th Street Tower, grumbled between two "cuts" of baggage cars, and was swallowed by the gabled griminess of old Dearborn Station.

Out of the corner of his eye, Martin detected a scraggly queue of welcomers, people strung out along the platform as he sidled *Super-2's* dirtied red nose up to the "bumper" for Track 5, set the air, clicked the throttle shut, turned off the dinging bell, and read "10:48" on his gold watch... TWO HOURS AND FIFTY-SIX MINUTES *ahead* of schedule... faster than any Santa Fe train had ever or would ever come into that venerable depot from California!

On top of its phenomenal elapsed time of 36 hours and 49 minutes at an *average* speed of 60.8 miles an hour for the 2,227.3 miles, *Super-2* could lay claim to another sort of record.

Out of the smoking reduction of schedule by *three hours,* one could, if one was of conjectural bent, subtract another *hour and fifty-six minutes* for the 17 stops they had made and come up with an ACTUAL running time of 34 hours and 53 minutes for the journey, or a possible *average* speed of *64 miles an hour!* For 1937, forty-two years ago, it's something well worth pondering retrospectively.

All trains ascending Raton Pass were required to have a helper engine on the head end. Eastbound trains picked up their helper at Raton, New Mexico, while westbound trains coupled on their helper engine at Trinidad, Colorado. In this view the *Super Chief* has just crested the summit of Raton Pass at Wootton. — R. H. KINDIG

15

Well, Santa Fe had its record—THE record—and the faces of the "brass" gathered below Martin's cab window that May 17th, 1937 morning showed their pleasure as obviously as children at holiday time.

"Go meet your public," Campbell chided his hesitant companion engineer, and good-naturedly pushed the stocky Southerner half-way out the side door and down onto the wooden platform to accept the plaudits of the knot of "brass" led by the road's President Bledsoe.

"Great run, J.W., great run," chanted the aging and ill head man as he pumped Martin's hand, a hand that would be stilled by death in just four short years. But that morning at Dearborn, that radiant May day, the thick set engineer was having his finest moment, his last *great* moment.

A pair of reporter-types (no photographers) from the *Tribune* and *Times,* plus a "remote" radio announcer, lingered at the perimeter of the executive welcomers and, more as an afterthought than anything else, stepped up to Martin, then joined by Campbell and Reeves, and asked his name. He gave it and on further questioning, allowed as how "this was just another run." A bit more prompting and he added, "it *was* kinda nice being the 'end man' on a show ride like this."

From out the vestibule door of *Taos*, in a rather tumbling array, "execs" erupted onto the board platform, shouting to friends and strangers alike. Then, fully aware that they were privy to a scrap of immortality, railroadically speaking, they behaved more expressively than upper echelon folk did ordinarily.

The leading "exec" of the seventy claimed, purring into a WGN microphone, "The smooth-riding qualities of this train and the quiet and ease with which it operates dispel all sensations of extraordinary speed."

Besides being stilted rhetoric, it was hog-wash ... then and now, brought on, no doubt, by the "on mike" gent who felt motivated to say something "nice" in return for Santa Fe's free bed-and-board on the trip to Chicago.

"Smooth-riding," yes. "Quiet and easy operating," yes. But "no sensation of extraordinary speed," hardly!

When *Super-2* slashed *three full hours* off an already ambitiously speedy schedule, the riders of that train, all of them, knew full well that they had been on board for one helluva run— no matter how good a condition the side-sway bolsters, springs, and right-of-way were in! Yes, indeed, *Super-2's* "execs" got quite a romp!

And so ended 14-days, four "preview" trips, and 7,284 miles of "goodwill" running for *Super-2*. For its benificent offering to the press, *literati*, and "big biz" of complimentary exposure to their flag-bearer, *Super-2*, before she went into regular, main-line service, Santa Fe shelled out something in excess of one hundred thousand dollars!

To point up, again, but one of the peripheral goodies on that "Press Preview" run to New Mexico, Santa Fe even provided automobiles for their author-artist guests. *That* was class ... 1937 class!

The public—the ordinary, every-day people—clamored to and did go on-board *Super-2* everywhere she was exhibited; that justified some of the road's expenses of exhibiting, but only minutely, really, because scant few of the 1937 public ever again got near *The Super*, let alone on-board her.

As far as that goes, the wined-and-dined free-riders did little to weight *The Super's* passenger manifest once trips were for keeps. *The Super*, let's face it, was made for and paid for by showfolk and day-in/day-out travelling businessmen. With them already in the fold, Santa Fe could just as well have saved its "hundred

One of the first photos taken by Stan Kistler was this scene of the *Super Chief* at Lamanda Park, just east of Pasadena.

thou'."

Back at Dearborn again, reminiscent of ocean liner arrivals in the old movies, everyone at the old station's Track 5 was gone. All of a sudden "execs," porters, reporters, Western Union boys, luggage carts, even the car inspectors had dispersed and what had, mere moments before, been the focus of all their eyes—*Super-2*—stood in metallic repose . . . its stainless sides dimmed with dust and streaked with the dried rivulets from rain storms back along the line. Water dripped haphazardly from just-used pipes, and steam murmured in lines under the cars.

In the Diesels' engine-rooms, Blickle and Golden—two bushed maintainers—tidied, puttered, and neatened things . . . checking further on what they'd have to do with No. 4 cylinder when they got to the roundhouse and, lo and behold, inspecting a very suspect *traction-motor*.

In the background, the voice of the train caller megaphoned in-and-out of the depot's drafty nooks and crannies. Slyly, a stubby steam engine puffed into the trainshed and, like a mother cat gathering her kittens, carried off the cars toward Corwith Yard. Freed of the train behind him, John Martin knocked the ashes from his pipe, swung around in his chair, and backed the road-weary—one-sick-cylindered—Diesels also toward the beckoning sanctuary of Corwith's rest-and-repair shops. The tang of hot oil from engines that had been running constantly for forty-some hours left an odorous trail along the length of Track 5 and all the way out to the roundhouse at 18th Street. What had surely been an electric instant was over.

The E 1A's rolled up to a hissing stop in front of the roundhouse, where Martin pulled his throttle to "idle," spilled just enough air to brake the two units, and dropped a yoke over the control-buttons to lock the power off the wheels. "She's all yours," Martin said, somewhat wearily, into the measured gazes of a pair of coveralled figures leaning against the ladder rails below him. Diesel maintainers Ray Milton and Lou Goodrich knew their way in and around and under those *Super-2* E 1A's about as well as any mechanics could know engines that were scarcely out of their infancy. In their hands, 2-2A could expect hard-nosed and yet very special care.

"Helluva run, John," the sober-faced Goodrich hollered up to Martin for openers. "We kep' track of you and the other guys all the way in . . . 'shame 'bout that damned piston but, hell, you still got here way ahead o' time."

"Thanks," Martin grunted in a flat tone, adding, "We gave 'em somethin' to shoot at alright," as he made his way down the ladder, headed for his '36 Chevy, and home.

It was late on a December afternoon when Otto Perry photographed the *Super Chief* easing away from the Albuquerque, New Mexico station. Albuquerque was sort of mid-point on the line and the cars were always thoroughly inspected there.

182

16

Having "met" Ray Milton and Lou Goodrich, it might be well to touch on what they and their uniquely able *confrères* did ... way back when.

The Super Chief Diesel maintainer was a very rare breed, the first and the last of his kind and, rather like the Pony Express rider, relatively short-careered.

On Santa Fe, at any rate, the maintainer came on the scene officially during the summer of 1935 when the road took delivery of its first *passenger* Diesels, 1 and 1-A, the first locomotives they'd have where engineer and engines were completely separated, not even visible to one another. According to the then-applying union rules, the fireman could not and would not attend to the actual power source. So, enter the maintainer, precisely that ... but more.

The maintainer primarily tended the engines *on-the-run* but, by the same token, watched over them at the terminals as well. In other words, the maintainer was much like an intensive care nurse: always beside his Diesel charges—watching, gauging, listening, and when the occasion demanded (which was often), administering life-support and tender-loving-care.

The *early* Diesels, again as they involved *The Super* and Santa Fe, were, according to the maintainers and engineers who pampered them, pleaded with them, railed at them, and knew them best, out-and-out monstrosities—undependable, underpowered devils—veritable mazes of potential troubles and aggravation, as often as not shut down and running ignominiously *behind* tried-and-true steam locomotives over many segments of the system.

Conversely, though, the maintainers' ledgers had a credit side, too. Those first road Diesels, they'll tell you, had plus factors. They were all but unchallenged as givers of horsepower for the fuel they burned, needed little water, and when in trim, ran *The Super* as eagerly and as audaciously as unruly children at-play. They could accelerate like mountain goats. They could rip, roar, and ramble. They could, and did, give Santa Fe's Premier Train a wonderfully picturesque, albeit occasionally inanimate, source of power.

The maintainer, then, torn between love and hate for his volatile, in-line equipment, was of necessity psychiatrist, wet-nurse, whipper, and hand-wringing guardian to those first *Super Chief* Diesels, cars of power but infested with "bugs"—nettlesome mechanical aberrations peculiar to any piece of unproven machinery.

The week-to-week life of a maintainer in those early days (1936-'37) of *Super Chief* Dieseling was rough-and-rugged duty—pure old-time, hours-be-damned railroading. Sometimes those mechanic-nomads would put in 65-70 hours continuous duty, "living" on *The Super*, going from Chicago to Los Angeles, stealing an hour or two of sleep, when they could, in their Pullman bunks in *Clover Knoll* or *Isleta*.

Arriving in Los Angeles on Thursday mornings, they'd stay on the Diesels and go straight to the Redondo Junction Roundhouse to get their regular, between-trips work done on the engines. After that, nearly every trip required a 60-mile-out, 60-mile-back trip to the San Bernardino shops to change-out wheels or maybe a traction motor. Redondo Junction, you see, hadn't the equipment to lift the power-units high enough, even on jacks, to do that sort of work.

Thus, all-day and all-night Thursday, the maintainers were at "Berdoo." Early Friday mornings, back they'd go to Redondo Junction, sign out, and by noon, with pretty nearly *67 hours* "on" the engines, present their drained-dry selves at LA's bifurcated Rosslyn Hotel for a hot bath and, if they were lucky, five or six hours' sleep in a real bed.

184

It wasn't any time, though, 'til the bleary-eyed maintainers were jangled awake at 6 P.M., splashed cold water on their sleep-sodden faces and, by half-past six, were at the LA Round-house . . . hoping against hope that they'd have their charges (one maintainer to each Diesel unit of 2-engines) purring contentedly and standing proudly by the time they got to La Grande Station at 7 P.M.

8:00 P.M. Fridays, *The Super* and its maintainers were off again, as if without respite, trundling out of Los Angeles for an almost 40-hour run back to Chicago, 5 or 6-hours' work at Cor-with when they got there and then, and only then, *home* Sunday night . . . the family, and blessed sleep.

Monday morning was usually given over to "mechanical" con-ferences at Santa Fe's offices or at one of the roundhouses there in the "Windy City." Lunch was taken on-the-run and the re-mainder of Monday they worked on the units . . . home again, hopefully, by "9."

Tuesday, the *day* at any rate, a maintainer might huddle with his stockbroker, mow a lawn, take in a movie, luxuriate in a hot tub, or just sit on his porch and nod to the neighbors. But by "6" he was on-duty, back at the omnipresent roundhouse, coveralled, capped, and at "7:15," sliding out from under Dearborn Station's roof aboard *The Super* . . . ready, or so he appeared, to do the whole thing all over again!

En route, it might interest the reader to know, the main-tainers—almost invariably busy in the always attention-demand-ing units—were served their meals, rather incongruously, on silver trays right beside the roaring engines or, not unusually, on the oily deck of the bucking gangway, the handsome silver tea-service jiggling crazily on the gleaming server . . . crazily but soundlessly under the deafening roar of the engines.

For those of mechanical bent, the maintainers could—right while *The Super* was rolling along at high speeds—change-out injec-tors, water pumps, sometimes do complete cylinder, piston, and rod assemblies, or, off the Diesels, perhaps most unpalatably, en-gage in bureaucratic badgering to arrange for steam-helper loco-motives to get *The Super* into town after not uncommon motor or axle-bearing failures. Besides what they did *in* the Diesels, maintainers had some rousing set-to's outside the units—things

185

that, by today's standards, would rank above or beyond the call of duty.

For instance, about 8:15 on a bitter cold, blizzardy night in November of 1936, westbound near Lupton, Arizona, *The Super-1*—with Clarence Chambers at the throttle—swept into a snow-curtained cut and plowed through a small herd of cattle. One of the cows went under the train, breaking off four steam heat conduits: two at the diner and another pair on the next-to-the-last Pullman. Chambers "poured sand" and ground to an icy stop, his lighted train all but obliterated in the blackness by whirling, stinging clouds of snow.

Maintainers Larry Brasher and Harry Gill and the fireman—damning all deities who supposedly watch over railroad men—plopped out of the warm engine rooms, into the driving snow, and slid beneath the big, ice-crusted steel cars. Armed only with flashlights, frozen tools, and carloads of guts, the three, lying on their backs between the rails in the snow and ice, changed-out the four steam heat conduits and thus kept the train from freezing, something that could have delayed *The Super* from 8 to 12 hours, maybe more.

As it was, the three men in their yeoman stint under the cars—in the icy dark with numbed fingers and backsides—"delayed" *The Super* only an *hour and twenty minutes*! What's more, they made-up an hour of that loss by the time they got to Los Angeles! Small wonder that the businessmen and the show-folk were so devoted to *The Super Chief*.

Rejoining the four maintainers and the newly-arrived record-setting *Super-2* Diesels, all gathered there in the hazy 1937 May-morning air outside Chicago's 18th Street Roundhouse, it took just a little more probing to confirm what Blickle, Golden, Milton, and Goodrich had suspected. Unit "2B" had indeed burned out a traction-motor. That, along with the "blown" piston and a questionable generator in "2," the lead unit, would, they all agreed, hold the red-nosed Diesel duo out-of-service next day for the first *regular* run of *Super-2*.

Almost in unison, the four maintainers looked across the roundhouse "apron" at two Diesels dozing in the sun . . . the flat-faced veterans 1 and 1-A that had brought the last *Super-1* in the day before. Right at that moment, desperately needing power and seeing as how they had only four road Diesels altogether, the gaudy 1 and 1-A looked as welcome to Santa Fe as two relief pitchers to a manager who had just taken out his last "starter." Typically, "1" had some bearing problems but, if you'll remember, "512" was back there at Newton so, in the next 31½-hours, they had ample time to run *it* "light" into Chicago to run with "1-A." So it was that "1-A" and "512" would haul the first revenue *Super-2* next day, the 18th of May, 1937.

The stage, then, powerwise, was set for *Super-2* to get out of Chicago. Across Corwith Yard, scrub crews were busily hand-washing the *Super-2* cars which, moment by moment, were losing their dirty "faces" and looking more and more like a gleaming rank of luxurious palanquins waiting to carry, in curtained and mattressed finery, their complement of 104 favored riders. As the only stainless steel equipment in the big yard that day, they shone all the more brightly and the nine corrugations at their waists sent off a dittoing of reflections. In that instance, however, as handsome and as exotic as *Super-2* was, there would be no observation car brightwork to foliate for a christening ceremony as was the case with *Super-1*.

17

A ctually, there wouldn't be really what one could call a christening "ceremony" for *Super-2* on May 18th, 1937. They wouldn't douse her with champagne, there wouldn't be any celebrities posing at the observation end, no speeches, no reporters, no flowers. . . . they would simply load her to capacity with show-folk, artists, writers, and businessmen and, without any flak-and-flame, send her off into the dusk and darkness.

It has always struck this writer as odd that a train as magnificent and as inarguably unique as *Super-2*—the loveliest that Santa Fe ever planned, bought, or ran—would be given such a run-of-the-mill send-off when the paying passengers got on. Obviously the road had invested so much *élan* into the *bon voyage* for *Super-1* and then the two weeks of press "previewing" and "good-willing" for *Super-2* that, when it came time to celebrate *Super-2* getting out of Chicago, they'd simply run out of "gas" for publicity.

In short, the hoopla for "regular" *Super-2* simply wasn't there. As we've already seen, even the Diesels were to be out-of-"sync" with the rest of the train's streamlined continuity for her maiden voyage. But in the places where it really counted, Santa Fe saw to it that *Super-2* would, by all means, be SUPER.

Observation lounge *Navajo* contained two Drawing Rooms, one done in Satinwood above powder blue upholstery and deep blue carpeting. (ABOVE RIGHT) The autumny tones of figured Red Gum set off the deep turquoise of fabric and copper colored carpeting in a Compartment in *Isleta.* — BOTH SANTA FE RAILWAY

In the kitchen-cupboards and refrigerators of *Cochiti,* in the liquor-cabinets of *Acoma,* in the linen-lockers of the sleeping cars, in the stationery racks—filled-fat with sand-colored note-paper with "*Super CHIEF* En Route" embossed on it in shiny black and scarlet—and certainly, in the "celebs" who would occupy its wood-rich staterooms and sections, *Super-2* was more than ready to begin a new era of opulence for its owners!

Not even the off-beat Diesels would really mar the overall *Super* patterning for, as a train, she was confluently rakish, in-nately well-designed, and most assuredly, never-to-be-dupli-cated. Even the nine waist-corrugations which we've alluded to several times were a one-of-a-kind design element.

As has also been previously mentioned, the curve configuration of the end of the observation car roof was used but once by its

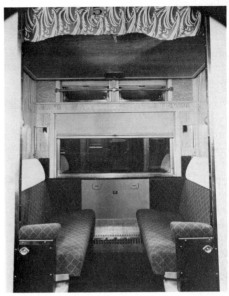

Peacock Green berth seats and Jade-and-Forest Green carpeting course through the creamy confines of Section-Sleeper *Laguna* under accenting crimson designs in the tan curtains overhead. (ABOVE RIGHT) Lightly Golden Avodire with its splash-mottling rides walls and berth bottoms over soft blue fabric, deep blue carpeting, and all below cream curtains with blue patterning in a Section in *Isleta*. — BOTH SANTA FE RAILWAY

builder. And the reader knows, too, that the *décor* of each and every stateroom was entirely different—architect Harbeson saw to that. But the *degree* of hand-fashioning has not, the writer feels, been adequately brought out. With the cars "in" the yard, here seems an opportune time to do so.

In no way is it even inferred that *Super-2* was the only train that had had custom care lavished on it. That was done back in the 1800's. Still and all, Harbeson and Company did pack more one-of-a-kind *hand*-crafted variety into those staterooms and sections than any assembly-line train could have hoped for. *Hand*-executed sand paintings by Sterling McDonald, *hand*-stitched fabrics and carpeting, *hand*-shaped bookcases, a *hand*-wrought turquoise-and-silver lamp with a *hand*-stretched goat-skin shade, *hand*-glued and *hand*-applied veneers, a *hand*-pa-

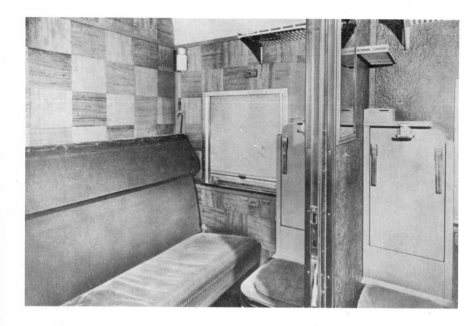

Adjoining Bedrooms in *Taos* reflected the Redwood Burl in the foreground with "checkerboarding" of Teak above persimmon upholstered couch in the room beyond. — SANTA FE RAILWAY

Photograph showing how the vestibule trap door and folding steps worked aboard one of *Super-2's* just finished stainless steel cars. — THE BUDD COMPANY

The pale tones of Aspenwood lend a delicate, almost fragile, grained background to the pebbly lemon yellow upholstery and citron carpeting of a Compartment in *Oraibi*. — SANTA FE RAILWAY

pered photo mural . . . name it and *Super-2* had it *hand*-done.

Hand-cut and *hand*-glued wood inlay, *hand*-sawn radio-speakers, light fixtures . . . on and on . . . item-after-item that made the seven cars of *Super-2* into what was virtually a *hand*-built entity. Here, forty years later, as has also been said before, she still stands unequalled.

For the remainder of May 17th and up until 6 P.M. of the 18th, *Super-2* was scrubbed, polished, and re-stocked with fresh linens and enough food and beverages to swell a hotel menu and wine-list. By 5 P.M. on the 18th, steward Peter Lombardi and chef Carlos Gardini had provisioned *Cochiti* in sumptuous fashion, picked-up their embossed menus, and at that very instant, had

Cochiti, 'neath an incandescent flesh dome, exuded a convivial, brownish-red warmth from its African Rosewood walls atop a rust-and-black carpeted stage. Damask napery fanned out in white stratae and orangey-red chairs punctuated that whiteness hotly. Yellow and gray striped shades, below satin-finished lighting tubes, gracefully softened and pulled together long spans of glass — aided by the cozying folds of desert sand drapes. Water-dropleted yellow rose buds were centered on each table to gentle the primitive satin-toned Mimbres Indian-patterned chinaware and silver service — much of it reflected in the peach-colored mirror above the Walnut buffet *sur entree.*

...ator and author Stan Repp. "This is strictly a sketch
...rain was in service only a few days. It was windy and
...nde station, pushing fifty then, stood like a big brick
...a true study in contrast."

the crew shaking out and laying-on the heavy, figured, Irish-linen tablecloths, atop which, in a silver vase at the window-end of each table, they placed a single yellow rose in a nest of delicate fernery.

The heavy, primitive silverware bordered the hand-painted china and the bright orange chairs shone from lusty rubbings with leather wax. The sand-colored drapes were pulled just a little closer together to heighten the coziness, and glassware was polished that "one more time." The peach-tinted buffet mirror was wiped "speck-free" and the walnut face of that buffet gave off a rich patina. Barrel-chested Lombardi, sanguine, no doubt, at the handsomeness of his colorfully impeccable diner, shouted in a thick accent, "Bring on the show folks!"

At "6," off they all went, backing toward Dearborn Depot, the juicy raisin pies already baking and bubbling in *Cochiti's* ovens. Walking the aisles among the staterooms, one got copious whiffs of the inimitable lineny fragrance of new bedding and the appealingly sweet, downy odor of dull-rose Pullman blankets.

Its lighting always vivified *Super-2* and, even though it was not yet dark, many of the shades were drawn to keep out the sun and thus permitted one fortunate enough to have been there a glimpse of the soft, subdued candlepower in the lounge, *Acoma*, the dazzling color-laden luminosity of the diner, *Cochiti*, the glaucometer blue of the stateroom "night" lights, and what may well have been the most alluring of all the train's illumination— the turquoisey aura of *Navajo's* Indian lounge, a fitting end to 562-feet and $560,054 worth to *elégance*.

By "6:15, *Navajo's* purple insignia snuggled up to the end of Track 5 and, with a sigh of air, she and her six companions— *Taos, Oraibi, Cochiti, Acoma, Laguna,* and *Isleta*—stood ready for duty. At the other end, faithful ol' "1-A" and newly-arrived "512," as we said they would, coupled-on under the subtle, long-practiced manipulation of Santa Fe's most senior engineer, Wesley Pledger McAfee, *49-years* on the engines! When the chunky, fatherly-looking, middle-sixtyish McAfee climbed down the side-ladder onto the greasy wooden platform to light a fresh cigar and clean his glasses, things had come full-circle for *The Super Chief*: just six-days over a year before that, Manley Marsh took *Super-1* out of Dearborn and into the passenger world. *What* a year it had been!

—⎯Super CHIEF

Navajo, even minus the wrapping of wood veneers in the other cars except, that is, in its Walnut-and-Birch magazine cases and writing desk — totally claimed one's color sense on sight! Here was a vibrant vault of turquoise swirling overhead almost like "sky" — held up by earthy copper walls draped in pebbly brown. The bluish-purple, red, and cream Bayeta chairs and settees rode the cocoa carpet as naturally as blankets on an Indian pony. Sand paintings done on cork, like the one shown on the right, bordered the 51-inch long windows and brought to mind the *hogan* . . . as did the lighted red tips of "plumed arrows" (lamps) set between the end windows. A goatskin-shaded silver "ceremonial knife" lamp at the last window a-glowing, gleaming final statement to that vividly and uniquely colored, curved galleria, a sanctuary for observing and conserving.— BOTH SANTA FE RAILWAY

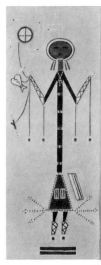

196

Sterling McDonald's sand paintings of four-skirted goddesses postured lengthily between blacks, blues, reds and yellows over a Walnut and Birch ebonized Mexican Parota magazine-case top . . . all lighted from Satin-finished open-finned "coves." Ash tray bases were "milk chocolate." —
BOTH SANTA FE RAILWAY

The Kachina-bar end of lounge car *Acoma* with its Bird's-eye Cypress upper walls and ceiling in light tan prima vera. — SANTA FE RAILWAY

"LIGHTS! . . . CAMERA! . . . ACTION!"

At 6:30, through the iron gates came the advance echelons of *Super-2's* first Hollywood-Broadway passengers. In the vanguard came the lumbering lankiness of black-haired, beetle-browed, 41-year-old sportswriter/novelist Paul Gallico, resplendent in a plum-colored houndstooth sport coat, azure slacks, and chartreuse "Ascot," arms awash with magazines, the "trades," and a half-dozen Lucky Strike "flat-fifties." The bespectacled Gallico, one could bet, would spend most of that maiden voyage slamming away at the typewriter, chain-smoking and lubricating his mental processes with liberal infusions of "Old Grandad."

Beside the loping Gallico, in striding incongruity, came Harvard man/poet Ogden Nash, conservatized in Ivy League tweeds

At the forward bulkhead end of *Navajo's* lounge was a deep purplish-blue chair set before a Walnut-faced desk and shelves positioned before a sepia-toned photo-mural of, most appropriately, Navajo weavers and their flock. The desk was stocked with red and black engraved train stationery printed on a soft desert-toned Bond paper. — SANTA FE RAILWAY

and a burgundy-red knit tie, freighting only a book-marked copy of James Robinson's *Human Comedy*. The round-headed Nash adored trains, as witness the first eight lines of his 1935 poem, "Riding On A Railroad Train:"

> *Some people like to hitch and hike;*
> *They are fond of highway travel;*
> *Their nostrils toil through gas and oil,*
> *They choke on dust and gravel.*
> *Unless they stop for the traffic cop,*
> *Their road is a fine-or-jail road,*
> *But wise old I go rocketing by;*
> *I'm riding on the railroad.*

A few yards behind Gallico and Nash, in a clicking concertizing of high-heels, two comely chorines from the Broadway "smash" *Babes In Arms* breezed-by in a perfumed panorama of *moiré* and *chiffon*, volleying verbal inconsequentialities, oblivious of the train, fellow-passengers, or anything else besides their non-stop monologizing.

Interspersed between the showgirls and a quartet of gray-flannel-suiters *schlepped* the double-breasted irrascibility of short, soft-bellied film-mogul Harry Cohn, bombarding a captive underling with atrabilious sentence-fragments out of the side of his consistently drawn-down mouth.

In Cohn's wake, mincing along in a flowered number fresh out of Sally Milgrim's, toting a tiny Underwood portable, came the New York *Evening Journal's* dollish, feisty, young-but-hardbitten show "biz" columnist, Dorothy Kilgallen—fresh-off a much-bally-hooed reportorial 24-day trip 'round the world (forty years ago, that was front-page copy!). Pert "Dorothy Mae," who had her own byline at eighteen, was Hollywood-bound to do re-takes for MGM's "Sinner Take All" and ferret-out newsworthy stuff—maybe even a "hot item"—for the column.

The "gang" was forming. In a chatterless lull, two coveralled car "tonks" came by and went about their endless peering and probing 'neath the cars. A pigskin overnight bag tumbled off a baggage cart and burst open, spewing a silken scattering of "Step-ins" onto the blackened veneer of the platform. Clumsy hands stuffed the filmy unmentionables back inside . . . hopefully unseen.

Poised at the vestibule to sleeper *Laguna* was five-feet-five-inches of cinnamon pin-stripe encasing the 225-pounds of renowned gourmand-cartoonist-train fancier George McManus, creator of "Jiggs 'n' Maggie." The roly-poly master of the pen-and-ink *mise en scène* in the comics chomped hard on a Maduro-wrapped cigar and inscribed circles in the air with a pearl-handled cane as he maneuvered his sybaritic girth up the steps and inside the car. Moments later, his fat-jowled face—cigar shifted to the furthest corner of his ample mouth—sat framed in a window mid-car, smiling broadly and waving to a friend with a black-covered sketchbook.

Long-shanked actress Charlotte Greenwood, fresh from an SRO run of "Leave It To Letty," followed McManus, hurrying along with that wonderfully airy gait of a Greyhound, 5'-10" of springtime in a turquoise blazer and snowy skirt-and-pumps that accentuated her engaging long strides.

Not more than four steps behind Ms. Greenwood came the delectably slender brunette Rochelle Hudson, star of Fox's "Mr. Moto Takes A Chance," angel-footing along in a big-brimmed buttercup "straw" and periwinkle Foulard frock, cuddling a bouquet of white rosebuds.

Slavic "march tones" next crept into the procession of *Super Chiefery* with the appearance of stolid Count Alexis de Sakhnoffsky, deposed White Russian, race-driver, automobile-stylist, and *Esquire's* resident expert on streamlining and hydro-dynamics—who ambled down the platform looking all the more bearlike in browns and tans.

A delightful change in counterpoint came perfumedly in the wake of the Count: the ivory Englishness of music-critic Lady Mabel Dunn drifted cooly beside *The Super* cars as she headed for her compartment in *Isleta*. Lady Dunn, as one would expect, hummed softly as she walked and, once at her car, spoke animatedly with Santa Fe's suave passenger traffic manager, William Black.—Oh, *how* the distaff side *did* brighten *The Super Chief*!

The pace of boarding quickened as it got toward "7," and the passengers were by then hot-footing it along the platform-boards. Buffalo *Times'* able air-brush artist, Tom McCoy, a Packard-fancier who drove as fast as he turned out his drawings, nearly jogged to refuge in *Oraibi*, his thin, sandy mustaches aquiver for one of Al Day's fine Martinis.

If we had avoided, for a moment, the cacophony of the platform and stepped on-board *Super-2*, we'd have bumped into Hollywood columnist "Beverly Hills," sitting beside a four-foot-plus window in *Acoma* jotting "exclusives" in a red Morocco Paramount script-binder, Remington portable poised and ready. Happily, later on, entrenched in a cottage at the Beverly Hills Hotel, "Bev" rated *Super-2* four "stars," and the legend rolled on.

—*Super* CHIEF

Back in *Navajo*, muffled talk leaked into the aisle from out of drawing room "C," soft musings from three men—noted magazine illustrators—who slouched opposite one another on the powder blue upholstery. Arthur William Brown, McClelland Barclay, and Russell Patterson were headed out to Paramount for finish-up "ad" drawings on the just-completed musical, "Artists and Models." Barclay, a hairy-armed man's man who painted the loveliest of ladies in the chatty pages of *Cosmopolitan*, fingered his mustache and cursed idly. Patterson, also mustached and a wavy-haired hell-raiser, puffed on a "Murad" and stared blankly out at the sooty rafters. Brown, "Brownie" to everyone, joined in laconically from behind oversize black horn-rims, complaining gently of the plethora of "beautiful gals" in Hollywood that made troublesome his task of selecting several dozen for the film.

The boarding procession and the sitting grew boring to Barclay, who unfurled himself, slapped his roommates on the knees, and wandered out into the corridor. "Let's have a drink," he gruffed back at the slumping pair, who brightened at the watering prospect and stretched out of their chairs in pursuit.

Two rooms down the way, they all paused to exchange bawdy insults with an owlish clump of a man in a battered red fez that rode over circular spectacles and a close-cropped little mustache. Gentled with a large box of chocolates that sat on the taupe cushion beside him, a torn-open carton of cigarettes astride the window sill, beak-nose buried in one of a littering of books, Alexander Woollcott was *Super Chiefing* west to huckster his "Second Reader" for Viking and visit some of his transplanted pals from the Algonquin "Round Table."

The trio of "Pulchritude Pickers," an alliterative Hollywood-ism given them by some wag at Paramount because they had, indeed, selected a bevy of beauties for "Artists and Models," meandered forward, stopping now and then beside a bedroom

Alexander Woollcott

here, a drawing room there, joshing cronies and promising get-togethers on-board or perhaps at the "Derby" after they got to the Coast.

Almost at train time, with the passenger-list of 104 just three short of "full," the stained old shed shrilled to extra life when trench-coated screen-idol Dick Powell, off to start work on "Hollywood Hotel," swept into view . . . pursued by a shouting, autograph-begging cluster of youngsters. Always the gracious traveller, Powell flashed his fabled grin and signed everything from books to timetables.

Unwittingly caught up in the pawing platoon of Powell autograph hounds was tanned, straight-haired, sportsy-type Ehret Loban Cord—from the classic car of the same name—Powell's travelling companion, from whom the singer would buy a jet black "Sportsman's Convertible Coupe" the day after *Super-2* got to Los Angeles. Yes, indeed, those Great Old Stars—they had flair!

Lost in the boisterous trailing-shuffle of Powell fans was the somber face of an old Chicagoan carrying—as though his life depended on it . . . and it did—a large but light suitcase. The dour face above a tan sharkskin suit belonged to Edgar Bergen, and the suitcase housed the irrepressible "Charlie McCarthy," both off to a June 1st opening at LA's "Coconut Grove."

Powell's coattails had no sooner cleared *Taos'* doorway than its steps snapped up-and-into place and its door slammed shut. Five-and-a-half other doors did likewise; the only one half-open was on *Navajo*, and out of it leaned the blue-coated torso of the rear brakeman, lantern up and waving.

"7:15." The cars moved faster and faster down Track 5, twitched abruptly to the right, and scurried off into the night on their way to California. Her two red tail lights and glowing purple medallion faded fast and were gone. *Super-2*, Wes McAfee at the controls of its unlikely Diesel combo, was at last on the timecard and headed into history.

A westbound *Super Chief-2* streaks along the flat countryside west of Ayer, Colorado, at 90 miles-per-hour. Locomotive No. 3A and 3B were added to the Santa Fe roster in January 1938. — OTTO PERRY

18

S*uper-2*, although it had no champagne send-off, did, all the same, carry away an illustrious band of passengers that May 18th, 1937, possibly *the* most name-studded she'd ever slip out of either terminal with. The author is glad he jotted-down the names and the costumes of some of them; glad, too, that he rode out to the Coast with them. It was unforgettable! A once-in-a-lifetime journey!

Super-2, its 104 first-riders caught in every situation in every part of the train, was hurdling the Des Plaines River for the second time when they chimed "first call to dinner." *Cochiti* that first night out, under the dominant hands of Peter Lombardi, an Italian who often masqueraded as French, was strikingly reminiscent of a dining *salon* on-board ship . . . the place where new passengers congregated and got to know or at least recognize one another. In that serendipitous Lombardi diner, under warm and largely indirect lighting, the filmland folk circulated in a riot of fabric finery ranging from the earthen sobriety of maroon to the eye-jangling collision of pomegranate and puce. That was the men!

Milady on *The Super* preened and postured in an even gayer garbling of the color-wheel—leaning toward melon greens, chemical blues and, in one bit of crashing spring frock palettery, al-

Red-hatted writer-singer Juliana Romm and her accompanist in the galleria of observation car *Navajo* the night of *Super-2's* first trip out of Chicago, May 18, 1937. — SANTA FE RAILWAY

izarin and ochre! The Broadway man-types sported a somewhat more subdued palette than the Hollywood *Super Chiefers*; still, their sartorial selectivity was anything but restrained. *The Super* "guys" from Manhattan favored one-shade suitings but their shirts, ties, and socks were a crowd-noise of color beneath stripes, dots, and any other geometric inscribings one could conjure up.

A wondrous example of the sort of male plumage that we've alluded to sat before a barricade of toast, chopped egg-and-onion and caviar, munching lemony bites of Malossol. Peter Arno—jut-jawed man-about-town and contributor to *Esquire* and *New Yorker*—fairly crackled in a Prussian blue shirt, white collar, and peppermint-striped silk tie. No question about it; the *Super-2* riders were decked-out that night! Even the usually somber-clad

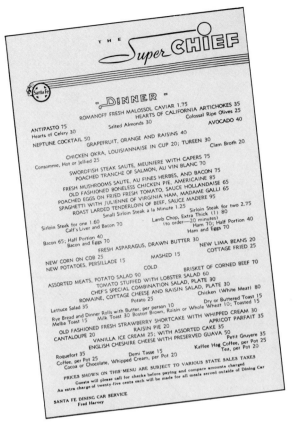

businessmen seemed caught up in the whirlpool of fashion frippery that *Super* inauguration-night and, here and there, a daub of bright hue livened-up the predominantly low-keyed commercial uniforms-of-the-day: sedate worsteds or the "ol' blue" serge that tonally disguised the wrinkles of travel.

Add to the winsome caprices of wearing apparel the warm backdrop of panelling and complementary culinary colorings and one has a rather good idea of the dinner-setting for *Super-2's* first revenue run. Into the sugar-icing, roseate glow of that boundlessly compatible scene, the miscible chef Gardini injected a spirit of "delish-and-delect" that, for the next twenty years of its life, wouldn't be repeated on *The Super*.

The hydrant-shaped *chef du chemin* roamed his tiny, utensiled bailiwick with the unbridled *joie de vivre* of a student cook on that May 18th night, the usual demeanor for Tuscan Gardini, reputedly *the* most capable chef of all those who rode the rails for

207

Fred Harvey. Marvelously inventive, Gardini, especially when seized by the *spirito Italiano*, could and did—right-then-and-there, in the hot, pitching diner, roaring along at "90"—create dishes of inordinate grace and flavor. His "stuffed Zucchini Andalouse," for example, could set even the "deli"-oriented tastes of Broadway and Hollywood atingle with delight.

Sometimes, for a very special patron, on the second night out—after they'd picked up their fresh trout at La Junta, Gardini would take a pair of the mountain beauties, done tender and flaky, *sauté* them with artichokes and mushrooms, and top the whole thing off with a luscious lime-butter sauce of his own concoction.

The broad spectrum of *Cochiti's* dinner-fare that first night was laudable. Intensely personal palatal praises of the feasting rang out, paeans from . . . Ziegfeld songstress Mitzi Mayfair, for a piping-hot tureen of "Pepper Pot" . . . from trencherman George McManus, an ecstatic hurrah for an oak-charred, inch-and-a-half thick chunk of "Chef's Special" sirloin . . . from explorer Attilio Gatti, for an ethereally puffy, buttery omelette bursting with fresh strawberries at the slightest pressure of his fork . . . from turbaned Mazo de la Roche, for a platter of delicate, sienna-brown breasts of capon, creamily and steamily bordered with nuggets of mushrooms à la king . . . from hotelman Ralph Hitz, for a lip-soft slice of finely-flecked, fat-edged, aged-just-so larded tenderloin, as rosy as if a child had colored it with a red crayon, rising like a blushing island out of a shallow pond of sanguine *sauce Madere* . . . from Dick Powell, for a nest of snuggling chips of *au gratin* potatoes, still bubbling under a pebbly, orange-and-brown veil of crumbs and cheese . . . from velvet-vested *Esquire* artist Gilbert Bundy, for a saucy wedge of *Super* hot apple pie, almost hidden beneath a craggy, big-as-a-hatchcover slab of cheddar . . . from 'round the world dasher Dorothy Kilgallen, for many cups of the blackest coffee, exuding shimmering surface droplets of brandy . . . and, after the dishes for her shad roe *sauté* were cleared away, from green-hatted vaudevillienne Ethel Shutta, for the bouquet of her *Chateau Latour '20*. Alexander Woollcott held court at his table, chain-smoking from a long onyx holder—between cigarettes, nibbling bits of choice *Petit Gruyere*.

208

Steward Lombardi toured inquiringly among his first-night guests, barrel-chest "out to here," brusquely pleased when they enthused, eyebrows pinched if they didn't . . . a powerful force in that oh-so-important 9¼x38-foot room where *The Super* passengers indulged in very necessary and, hopefully, satisfying moments of a twenty-two-hundred-mile journey. The old axiom "good food, good trip" seldom applied more pointedly than it did on *The Super Chief.*

Quartered, as they were, in space little more than minimal—luxurious, but all the same, minimal—confronted with countryside that was largely repetitive (if not at the beginning, it soon became so), and, being folks who were inclined to *nosh, The Super* passengers' thoughts were, by conditions and by nature, directed inward, literally and figuratively. And because its patrons were of means and accustomed to preferential treatment—besides being, as Noël Coward put it, "highly strung"—the prospect of dining on *The Super*—sometimes just getting up and mingling—loomed far more appealing to its largely celebrity *clientèle* than it did to the average train-travelers.

As we've said before, *The Super* diner was, in addition to its primary function, a place in which to feed the ego as well . . . and was there ever—outside of money, of course—a dearer word in the lexicon of the *dramatis personae* of Broadway and Hollywood than "self?" So it was then that Santa Fe, Fred Harvey and, by all means, the stewards and chefs who staffed it, catered to the whims and wants of the *Super Chiefers* with devotion (not always pleasure) above and beyond the call of duty.

Lombardi, in spite of his *bravura* and even occasional Latin irritability, was most solicitous to his "biz-and-show-biz" passengers, and coddled them with his enormous, tough, but ever-so-indulgent hands.

Coddling and catering on *The Super* diner took on more tangible forms, too—for example, in the special foods, or maybe to phrase it more accurately, the different foods that were put on board or kept aboard for "regulars," or in some cases, to sate ethnic leanings. Two items that did not always appear on *The Super's* menus but were nevertheless invariably in the larder when the train left either terminal were kippered herring and fresh mackerel.

Long-time *Super Chief* chef-steward Eddie Dyke recalled recently that the herring ("kippers") were served on slices of charcoaled toast, usually with a creamy batch of scrambled eggs and, if the passenger wanted a tangy touch, thin slices of raw onion topped with a sprinkling of capers. The mackerel enjoyed dual preparation . . . broiled to-a-turn with a "wreath" of bay leaves riding fragrantly on its charred surface, or pan-broiled and set amongst a bed of frosty parsley, lemon "wheels," and a flanking *cordon* of boiled new potatoes, lightly salted and dripping butter.

Pheasant on-board *The Super* was delectable and served, uniquely enough, atop a partially hollowed-out half-loaf of bread that had been plunged into deep fat—like an enormous French fry—serving as a golden brown bed for the succulent game bird. *Garni* of watercress verdantly emcompassed the ennobled fowl, which the all-knowing floated heavenward with a bottle of *Lanson Père et Fils, '26.*

Cochiti's third dinner-seating was thinning out by the time *Super-2* flashed in and out of Surrey, Illinois, and the eighteen or twenty left at-table dispersed in something of a flurry, heading forward alongside the kitchen to take up perches in the cool, dim-lit, goldenly zebra-wooded confines of the next car, the lounge *Acoma.*

In contrast to the diner that fairly dazzled with color and conversation, *Acoma*, despite a capacity crowd, had an ice-cube-clinky air of serenity about it. Brashness diminished and a clubby intimacy settled over the room. Champagne was "on the house" that inaugural night, a gesture of amelioration, no doubt, for not having had a bottle-breaking ceremony back at Dearborn depot. Whatever the motivation, "bubbly" spritzed-and-sparkled in nearly every glass except, that is, the ones of the no-nonsense imbibers.

For the heavy drinkers, *Super-2's* First Night Out just might be a hard memory to dredge up—the night as well as the impromptu "Off to Buffalo" that The Three Rines—an arrestingly graceful vaudeville soft-shoe trio—were doing between the front of the bar and the pigskin settees . . . no doubt the only time it was ever performed at 90-miles an hour. Charlotte Greenwood, caught up in the improvisational terpsichory of the Messrs. Rine, shucked off her kid pumps and did a series of the high-kicks for which she was famous—all of it reminiscent of the unfettered frisking in Noël Coward's "I Went To A Marvelous Party." Table-hopping, though not easy at the speeds *Super-2* was making, was the order of the night, with clouds of film-talk and show-talk rid-

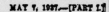

Liquor Board Bills Approved

Measures Would Give Office $800,000 for Additional Salaries

SACRAMENTO, May 6. (AP)—The Senate Committee on Finance today recommended for passage two bills which call for appropriations of $400,000 each, the money to be used by the State Board of Equalization in payment of salaries.

One measure by Assemblyman Robertson calls for $400,000 to be used by the board in adjusting salaries of the lower paid auditors in the sales tax division and in the employment of sixteen additional auditors for the Los Angeles district.

The other bill by Senator Swing provides for $400,000 for the liquor division.

Meet journalism's forgotten man. He sees nothing, tells all and his chief claim to fame and salary is his ability to write. Read "Rewrite" in next Sunday's Times.

Announcing the *entry into service of the superb* new *Super* CHIEF

May 21st

● On Friday, May 21st, a new Super Chief—new from headlight to tailsign—replaces Santa Fe's first Super Chief, that a year ago inaugurated 39¾ hour service between Los Angeles and Chicago ● The new train is of stainless steel, streamlined, Diesel drawn, air-conditioned. Here is the first streamliner built exclusively for first-class extra-fare travel ● The new Super Chief is broader and roomier inside than standard; smooth-riding; superbly appointed. Drawing rooms, compartments and bedrooms may be used singly or en suite. There are upper-berth windows, radio, clocks ● Unique is the varied use of rare and beautiful wood veneers; the application of Indian motifs to cocktail and observation lounges, and the cheery Fred Harvey diner, with its especially created silver and china ● As before, the Super Chief will leave Los Angeles each Friday evening, arrive Chicago 1:45 p. m. Sunday; leave Chicago Tuesday evening, arrive Los Angeles Thursday at 9:00 a. m. ● THE daily CHIEF—Supplementing the once-a-week Super Chief is Santa Fe's famous 49-hour Chief, completely air-conditioned, many-hours-fastest and only extra-fare solid-Pullman DAILY train between California and Chicago.

EARLY RESERVATIONS ON BOTH THE SUPER CHIEF AND CHIEF ARE HIGHLY DESIRABLE.

SANTA FE TICKET OFFICES AND TRAVEL BUREAUX
743 South Hill Street and Santa Fe Station, Phone MUtual 0111, Los Angeles ● 6405 Hollywood Boulevard, Hollywood ● Santa Fe Station, Pasadena ● 212 Santa Monica Blvd., Phone 265-86, Santa Monica ● 107 So. Brand Blvd., Glendale ● 117 Pine, Long Beach ● 132 W. Main, Alhambra

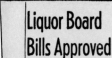 RESORTS 🚂 HOTELS 🎩 TRAVEL

The *Los Angeles Times* for May 7, 1937 carried this advertisement about the first eastbound run of the new all-streamlined *Super Chief* which would sail from La Grande Station on Friday evening the 21st of May. The notice also went on to mention that the daily *Chief* supplemented the once-a-week *Super Chief* on a 49-hour schedule.

Super-2, the all-streamlined version, is about to cross the Los Angeles River just prior to its on-time 9:00 A.M. scheduled first arrival at La Grande Station on May 20, 1937, as the text points out, behind Nos. 1 and 512 (the General Motors demonstrator). — GERALD M. BEST

ing the air on cigarette smoke and the vapors of *Pol Roger '26.*

—*Super* CHIEF

A near-eleven pause at Shopton, Iowa went entirely unnoticed by the *Acoma* loungers; chatter didn't subside for so much as a second.

The two chorines we "saw" back at Dearborn were, by the time *Super-2* got to Shopton, amply liquored and deep in *tête-à-tête* with a monocled old Gauleiter, a producer from Leni Reifenstahl's Berlin studios, here "on business." The only "business" that the Fatherland moviemaker was going to do with those two would be wine-and-dine them for a day-and-a-half—all the while getting specious answers and mascara'd flutterings to the raft of questions he would ask, perhaps even whether they had "relatives in Germany?"

The Super, almost from the very first day she ran, had an international reputation, and it was rather to be expected that she would attract, and did, in short order, carry more than her share of cosmopolite cargo . . . *Geheime Staatspolizei* included.

There was another visitor from the Continent on that inaugural *Super Chief* . . . scholarly, painfully shy Colonel don Alejandro Goicoechea, a Spanish Army officer-engineer who would, four years later, design and build the caterpillar-shaped "Talgo" train. Goicoechea, in his ill-fitting uniform and *capote militar*, was here for a look-see at how U.S. streamliners were put together—most especially, Cortlandt T. Hill's revolutionary Pendulum Car, then abuilding out in L.A.

The perpetually downcast Falangist inventor, only days away from war-torn Iberia, scrunched down in a deep rose-colored armchair, incredulous at the numbing disparity between the eye-filling *Super* lounge he was sitting in and the awful tawdriness of the trains in the homeland he had just left. But no matter how impressed the good Don may have been with *The Super*, his *Tren Talgo*, when he designed it in '41 and unveiled it late in '42, would be the barest of bare-bones inside of what was literally a miniature entomological casing.

At the reading-and-writing end of *Acoma*, arguing the relative but nebulous merits of two Greenwich Village bistros where they had lunched the day before, master wood cut artist-author-explorer Rockwell Kent and writer-early activist Lincoln Steffens good-naturedly stepped on each other's lines. Kent sitting "side-

213

saddle" at the desk and Steffens leaning across from a window chair were vociferous in supporting "Romany Marie's" and the "Pepper Pot." "Marie's" 55 Grove Street celebritarium won out, mainly by virtue of Kent's stronger vocalizing.

The talk in *Acoma* went on far into the night, and lights from most of the staterooms and both lounges glared long into the rushing darkness. Wes McAfee had a wide throttle on the Diesels as *The Super* roared along the "Race Track" toward Kansas City. Out around Marceline, ground-fog swallowed-up *Super-2*, her airhorn moaning an eerie, fast-fading "good night" from somewhere in the mist.

—*Super* CHIEF

Super-2, from its May 18th inauguration, had the "stage" all to itself for just a little over nine months—279-days, to be exact. It was time in which the transitory hours were kind to her and the very newness of her was almost protective. The cars kept their factory-freshness, the stainless facade showed few "dings" and sparkled healthily, and she ran on a schedule all her own. Inside, the panelling bore minimal scratching, finger marks, or other manifestations of transcontinental wear-and-tear . . . including smears from Wildroot or Brylcream hair lotions. Upholstery had retained all but a little of its original nubbiness, drapes were not yet faded, and leather couches and chairs were still pliable and relatively free of "cracking." The silverware had shed little of its sheen and the Coulter china glowed warmly and kiln-fresh. Even a few "new" smells lingered surreptitiously here and there, although conversely, things like the creaks of untravelled structure and "stiff" running gear had quickly gotten worked-in and no longer "spoke" new to the passengers.

Super-2 was, in short, from every aspect that one would choose to look at it, THE *Super Chief* of them all . . . the train to which all others in the line would be compared and, no matter what sort of improvements or innovations (radio and recordings in every room, train newspapers, Turquoise Rooms, etc.) that Santa Fe would put in or on its later models, *Super-2* was *the* touchstone for everything *Super* that came after. Those of us who were privileged to have ridden aboard her in the first months of her life were indeed fortunate—once-in-a-lifetime fortunate.

The new *Super Chief-2* at the same location as on page 212; however, the new Diesel power is included in the consist. Note the old standard Pullman car *General Hancock* in the consist. — GERALD M. BEST

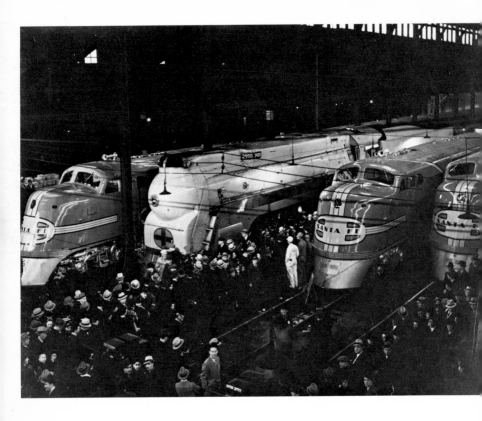

Streamliners for 1938

It was a frosty Saturday morning — February 12, 1938 — in the drafty train shed of Chicago's old Dearborn Station when Santa Fe, like any proud parent, lined-up for display to an over-coated crowd four of her newest racers. Left to right, Diesel No. 3 and the *El Capitan;* steam-styled steamer No. 3460 and the *Chief;* Diesel No. 6 and *Super-2;* and Diesel No. 5 on another section of the *El Capitan.* The *Chief* became a daily all-streamlined and all-Pullman train on January 31, 1938. Six complete train sets were required to make the daily schedule. The train was handled by steam power until after World War II. The *El Capitan,* an all-coach streamliner, sailed from Los Angeles and Chicago twice weekly beginning February 22, 1938. Two complete train sets were required to meet this service. — SANTA FE RAILWAY

216

The following day, the 13th, *Super-2* was still in town so, before sending the four trains of the previous day back up to Dearborn, the Santa Fe stood *Super-2* alongside its younger sisters and, with all five posing in the Chicago Terminal sun, gave the Inland Photo Service photographer *carte blanche* to "shoot" their panorama of just-delivered trainery — front and back. (ABOVE) Left to right, Diesel No. 2 of *Super-2;* No. 5 of the *El Capitan;* No. 3460 on the *Chief;* No. 3 on the second *El Capitan;* and No. 6 on *Super-2½.* (BELOW) The observation ends of (left to right) *El Capitan; Super Chief-2;* the *Chief; El Capitan;* and *Super-2½;* at the far right. — BOTH SANTA FE RAILWAY

217

for 1938

Santa Fe presents

AMERICA'S LARGEST FLEET OF ULTRA-MODERN STREAMLINED TRAINS

of 1938, regular Chicago ice be- most odern any

am ng rs s.

...ent it becomes pos... ...Chief. Twice-a-week service on the ...Chief; to re-dress the famous daily Chief on an equally high plane; to inaugurate a revolutionary new transcontinental twice-a-week economy train, El Capitan, to supplement the service of the popular daily Scout; and to present new streamlined service of exceptional convenience between Chicago and Kansas City, and Los Angeles and San Diego.

THIS, TOO, IS IMPORTANT. For two years, as an essential part in this great program for finer western transportation, Santa Fe has been improving roadbed, laying heavier steel, cutting down grades and straightening curves. Those of you who ride with us in 1938 will enjoy the smooth, quiet sweep of Santa Fe trains.

It is our high aim to render service that will bring Santa Fe new friends, and bind our old friends more closely to us.

Passenger Traffic Manager
Santa Fe System Lines

Another Superb

Super Chief

The Super Chief is the only extra-fare, streamlined, 39 3/4 hour train between Chicago and California, equipped and reserved entirely for first-class passengers.

The first streamlined Super Chief was placed in service May 12, 1937, on a once-a-week round trip schedule. Its popularity was immediate and spontaneous, and it has since been booked to capacity, in season and out. Hence our pleasure in announcing the doubling of this supremely swift, luxurious and convenient service. Commencing February 22, 1938, the Super Chief will leave Chicago twice each week, on Tuesdays and Saturdays at 7:15 P. M.; arrive Los Angeles Thursdays and Mondays at 9:00 A. M. Eastbound, departures from Los Angeles will be Tuesdays and Fridays at 8:00 P. M., arrival Chicago at 1:45 P. M. Thursdays and Sundays.

● This new Super Chief consists of nine cars, streamlined in stainless steel behind a 3600 H. P. Diesel-electric locomotive. It presents Fred Harvey service in its dining car, cocktail-lounge car, and baggage-club car. Accommodations include drawing rooms, compartments and bed rooms, for use singly or en suite; the new roomettes, economical and comfortable, and open sections.

● The second Super Chief is a fit companion to the first, heretofore considered by many the most beautiful train on American rails.

The Santa Fe Railway prepared this special brochure to *announce* all its new trains for 1938. — DONALD DUKE COLLECTION

19

Ordinarily, one would, I think, expect a logical progression of things and figure that, after *Super-2,* Santa Fe would come out with *Super-3.* Not so. To correct an occasionally held misconception, *Super-3*—as an entity—was not put-in-service on February 22, 1938. *Super-2,* rather, right in its regular turn, went west that day.

"2," a modified "2," lined-up at Dearborn on that frosty winter night when a new layer of crackly snow blanketed Chicago. To those hurrying passengers knowing enough, or perhaps we should say, caring enough to look, the one noticeable absentee from the original *Super-2* car-pack was lounge car *Acoma. Acoma,* you see, had been built without a shower-bath—an oversight, we'll assume, on the parts of its owners, designers, and builders that remains to this day unfathomable, especially when one thinks back to how much importance Santa Fe placed on the bathing-room ever since they put one on their first all-Pullman flyer, *The Deluxe.* A nine-month-showerless *Super-2* still confounds car-buffs and old passengers alike!

At any rate, on that nippy February night Santa Fe righted its laving wrong with a bang, for standing in *Acoma's* customary spot was a spanking new lounge car, *Agathla,* fresh out of the Budd-works and boasting a ladies' shower and a "beauty shop" to boot. Not content with offering one shower, Santa Fe had tucked in, up at the head end, a gleaming new Budd baggage-lounge car, *San Acacia*, which housed a shower room for the men right alongside a colorful barber shop, all done-up in rust-and-cream with a commodious pigskin Koken chair.

The railroad could well expect and did encounter a batch of reservations for sudsing, toweling, and cologning by its *Super-2* celebrity-riders, who had always put a heavy demand on barbering, lathering, and Pinauding . . . grooming prompted, in large measure, by two-thousand-two-hundred-and-twenty-eight miles of free time.

Super-2, then, ladies' and men's showers warm-and-waiting with stacks of heavy, oversize towels to wrap one's self in, was ready for hot bathing over the long, icy road west. And still there, parked at Dearborn depot, two of the ladies were already in the beauty parlour, one getting a pre-dinner "touch-and-comb" to her Marcel, the other, repairs to nails damaged in rugged action at-table that afternoon in "The Pump Room."

Lounges and showers weren't the only additions to *Super Chiefing* that February night. Nuzzling behind *San Acacia* was *Tuba*, a pleasantly pronounceable 17-roomette car just up from Cottage Grove Avenue and the *first* Pullman-built car put into *Super-2*.

In one move, then, Santa Fe had restored an old amenity—the bath, offered m'lady a beauty parlour, and increased its payload to 121. Nice correcting!

By "7:15" that February 22nd, 1938, growing windier, Chicago windier, all of *Super-2's* "121" were aboard, cozy and warm and edging out into the howling night, bound for salubrious and soothing climes. The moment that *Navajo's* "tail" got out from under the Dearborn shed, her lighted purple emblem was obliterated by a swirling cloud of snowflakes, off and gone in the white night.

—*Super* CHIEF

For some reason, lost in the murky niches of over forty years, there had been a delay at Pullman-Standard, and the six cars that they were building for *Super-3* in the early part of 1937 (*Chimayo, Talwiwi, Tyuonyi, Tchirege, Tsankawi,* and *Puye*) weren't ready by February 26th, 1938, the day actually targeted for releasing *Super-3* and initiating twice-a-week *Super* service.

In early 1937 Pullman-Standard began the construction of the streamlined cars for *Super Chief-3*. The six cars weren't ready for the targeted release of twice-a-week service on February 26, 1938. The cars included *Talwiwi*, a sleeper as shown above. In the view below the sleeper *Chimayo*. — BOTH PULLMAN-STANDARD

The sleeper *Tyuonyi*, with the upper berth windows visible above the letterboard. — PULLMAN-STANDARD

Pullman-Standard's *Super-3* cars, besides being late coming out, were totally—well, almost totally—different from the Budd-built *Super-2* equipment. Moreover, Pullman-Standard did not build all of *Super-3:* Budd turned out its lounge *(Agathla),* its diner *(Awatobi),* and its baggage-lounge *(San Acacia),* the latter, as we've said, a new-type of car in *Super Chiefing.*

The biggest difference between the Pullman-Standard cars and the Budd cars that preceded them lay in their basic structure and most noticeably, in the interior finishing. As a matter of fact, except for its overall outside dimensions, wheel diameters, and a few other manifestations of standard-gauging, plus the bulk of the lounge *décor* in *Puye,* the P-S *Super-3* was worlds apart from *Super-2!*

For starters, the P-S *Super-3* was foundationed and framed out of carbon steel ... just the exterior sheathing was stainless, and even that was differently patterned in its sectioning from Budd's configuring. Small chance, then, that "2" and "3" would be confused when seen from the outside and, heaven knows, most assuredly never from inside except, as we've said, in *Puye's* solarium lounge ... a valiant attempt, it must be admitted, by P-S to emulate *Super-2's* "ob" lounge in *Navajo.*

Here, and just for a moment, we can enumerate portions of the variances in "2" and "3." Pullman-Standard's *Super-3* had conservative *painted* walls (no panelling), conservative upholstery and carpeting, conservative windowshades, and perhaps most drearily—in areas so in need of a little sparking up—conservatively-colored fixtures in the lavatories. Indeed, *Super-3* was conservatism on wheels and, with that take-no-chances third *Super*—even the Budd cars on it had lost their *Super-2* sprightliness and careful customcrafting—a bit of the *Super* architectural flame flickered out for those of us who admired, nay, reveled in the full-blooded, woodsy, brightly-shaded, warm-'n'-wonderful *Super-2.*

Outside, however, on the *Super-3* cars, in the plates centered at their waists, all conservatism vanished as lettered pandemonium took place in eight of the nine names that vibrated off of them like a geological rollcall. The names were the ones listed a few paragraphs back, names that the author, again in the clutch of charitability, once called "tongue-twisters ... but also eye-catchers." In all truth, the eight—including *Puye,* which tickled yard crews, train crews, and passengers alike, and invariably

The Pullman sleeper of the new *Super-3* order from Pullman-Standard also included the *Tsankawi*. — PULLMAN-STANDARD

Budd-built diner *Awatobi* as shown at the 8th Street Coach Yard at Los Angeles. This view shows the dining section with the wide windows and the hallway next to the kitchen with the small windows. — STAN KISTLER

came out "Poo-ey"—were all but unpronounceable, aggressively so, and had none of the soft, Southwestern linguisicity or melifluity of the seven on *Super-2.*

With the larger part of *Super-3* not ready for its February 26, 1938 "coming out," Santa Fe had to send off something from Chicago on that blustery, bristling-with-icicles Saturday. Fortunately for the folks at 80 East Jackson, Pullman-Standard *had* delivered all of the contracted *Chief* equipment, so Santa Fe simply dipped into—borrowed from, if you prefer—the sixth train of that new *Chief* equipment, what was commonly referred to as the "protection" train . . . cars on stand-by in the event something went awry with any of the five trains it took to operate the *Chief* on a daily basis. Thus, the designation *Super-2½.*

Subbing for the uncompleted portion of *Super-3* still on the fabricating tracks at Pullman-Standard, Santa Fe coupled-up another team of cars bristling with Indian-flavored, Indian-only-pronounceable names—phonetically spelled at that!—out of Roger Birdseye's notebook, and on a bitter cold, snowy, late-February 26th afternoon, shunted their ice-draped bodies and wheels up into the scant protection of the draft-ridden shed at Dearborn Station. There, exhaling hot "breath" from every outlet, they set out for all to wonder at (fleeting wonder, needless to say, on that day), *Chinle, Wupatki, Klethla, Agathla, Awatobi, Polacca, Yampai,* and the observation car, *Chaistla,* its fastened-on *Super Chief* medallion already encrusted with clods of snow. The names alone, it scarcely need be said, conjured up enough of the sunny Southwest to warm the coldest hands of its hurrying, shivering, bundled-up California-bound passengers.

The *Chief* was "unprotected" that darkening, freezing afternoon . . . but a *Super Chief* would leave as promised!

So then, for five months (February 26th–July 2nd, 1938), *Super-2½* ran—six borrowed cars and all—fast-and-full over the system, giving its half of splendid, wide-ranging, twice-a-week service out-of-Chicago to *The Super's* "big biz" and "show biz" patrons.

Using that service, one could leave Chicago of a Tuesday night, be in Los Angeles 9 A.M. Thursday, do business that day and Friday, *Super* out Friday night, be in Chicago early Sunday afternoon, catch *The Century* out of there Sunday afternoon late, and be in New York—ready for business again—at 9 or 9:30 Monday morning. Even on a round-trip basis with an extra leg to Manhattan thrown in, a businessman would, out of the five-and-a-half days we've just noted, still lose only *one* business day, precisely as Santa Fe had dreamed ... and better!

Starting west again, this time using the other half of *The Super* twice-weekly service out of Chicago, the time-conscious could leave Chicago Saturday night, be in L.A. Monday morning, do business there Monday and Tuesday, and leave La Grande Depot for Chicago Tuesday night at "8:00." That was fine; only a day lost.

On the eastbound leg, however, *Super* riders lost not only the "one business day" but part of another as well (nearly four hours of it).

Summing-up, then, out of the four round-trips that the *Super Chiefs* made each week, only that Tuesday night trip out of L.A. "cost" its riders more than the promised "one business day" and even then, it was only 3 hours-45 minutes. Forty years ago, no matter how one viewed it, *Super* service was quite something!

Admittedly, it is rather far along in the *Super Chief* story to broach this point, but nonetheless, some of the readers might, about this time, be wondering why, at all, did businessmen and show people take *The Super*? Well, one might first stop and consider that, though it was only forty-some years ago in time, 1937 was, on the other hand, eons ago in the realm of transportation sophistication. In those days, the dreary mid-Thirties, the run between Chicago and the Coast was a two-option journey ... plane or train, period.

Parenthesizing for a moment, to persons of means, standing, and reputation—business and showfolk—the bus was unthinkable—an anathema—and the automobile, then short-ranging and hard-driving, was only slightly more palatable. About the automobile, the journey westward was, in the Thirties, to those who could have afforded to ride *The Super,* an out-and-out adventure needing ample time and a larking attitude toward the exigencies of the highway. When they went by car, the well-to-do—not the businessmen or show people—did their Chicago–L.A. autoing in chauffeur-driven *Isotta-Fraschinis, Pierce-Arrows* or big, brawny *Dusenbergs* ... comforted with picnic-hampers of squab, prime rib, and decanters of vintage wines or carafes of steaming Brazilian coffee. But—those jaunts were rare, rare indeed!

225

The writer is again assuming, and wrongly, of course, that the reader under fifty knows that, in the Thirties, long-distance automobile travel out west was, from mid-November to the beginning of May, for Chicago or L.A. destinations, all but out of the question! That left only the blistering summer for driving—business driving—and that was equally agitative for anyone, as we've said, but the most venturesome. Business, show or otherwise, went on *all-year.*

"Scratch" two, then, of the "alternatives" for getting between Chicago and the Coast. Back to the two reasonable options for making the trek . . . airplane or train.

The commercial airplane, as late as 1935, two-winged, tiny, and not deserving of the suffix "liner," was, to be sure, an uncommonly speedy means of getting between Chicago and L.A. in 1937—speedy and, in a few cases, handy. Oh, but it did have its faults. "Condors," "Tri-Motors," "Vegas," and DC-2s and "3s" were rough-flying, low-flying, noisy, and—talk about cramped! Although speed—time, if you will—was *the* selling point for getting on an airplane forty years ago, flying in those days demanded what this writer used to call the "Three D's" . . . dedication, docility, and when landing in a blinding snow or rain, derring-do. Not everyone had the "Three D's!"

Lacking radar and the multiplicity of refined instrumentation we now have, needing sometimes to make as many as three, maybe four landings—often snow-blinded, thunder-rattled, and daring touchdowns—between Chicago and the Coast, the "commercial" airplane in 1937 was not all that it had been made out to be: speed, yes; pleasantries, no!

Small wonder, then, that the knowing business traveller, the traveller who valued his sense and sanity even above and beyond the hurly-burly of big deals, contracts, and the machinations of commerce, toted-up the travel odds and settled, not lightly by any means, on the train . . . not just any train but, most happily, I'd wager, THE train . . . *The Super Chief.*

Taking *The Super* in '37 or thereabout was not at all the "last resort" prospect it might be today—were it still running. *The Super* schedule in those early, early days was a quite respectable piece of timing; the accommodations were pure *classe premier;* one felt safe aboard her no matter the weather outside. She offered time to relax or work, or most appealingly, move about in spaces and places that were handsomely, even lavishly decorated.

Conviviality reigned in her ample lounges and diner; *hâute cuisine* was the order of every meal; the best of wines and "well" whiskey were always on-tap; and there was, while in her staterooms, a much needed respite from telephones and attendant bothers.

The case as presented for the train—*Super* train, that is—may not have been a substantial one, nor will its arguing ever induce anyone to ride the rails. It's too late for that. What it might do, though, is score some latent points for a rather nifty part of mobile Americana and ideally, from the writer's standpoint anyway, cause the reader (the aerophile included), to say, aloud if he chooses, "Wish I'd ridden *The Super*—musta been a ball."

Having, so to speak, put the cart before the horse and already told about *Super-2½* and *3*—named their cars, told who built them, and laid bare the ins-and-outs of why they were put on, little need be said about the first trip of "2½" and its departure from Chicago.

In essence, *Super-2½* lined up at Dearborn depot in the early evening of February 26, 1938—the cars, as already pointed out, *San Clemente, Chinle, Wupatki, Klethla, Agathla, Awatobi, Polacca, Yampai,* and *Chaistla,* were lighted and inviting—ready to travel. It was another frosty night in Chicago and pretty much the same things went on boarding the passengers, sounding the "Highball," and on the dot of 7:15, gliding out into the freezing stillness and heading west. The only thing that might bear repeating is that, with *Super-2½*'s leaving, twice-weekly *Super* service out of Chicago began!

Super Chief-3 received new motive power in 1941 when Nos. 50-A and 50-B were received from the American Locomotive Company. Each unit was 2,000 hp. and are shown here at Corwith Yard, Chicago. — SANTA FE RAILWAY

20

The winter days of '38 gave way and slipped into spring. Summer bloomed hot and humid, and it wasn't long 'til Friday, July 1st rolled around. That day, Pullman-Standard finished up its part of *Super-3*, called for an engine from the Chicago Outer Belt Line, and delivered *Chimayo*, *Talwiwi*, *Tchirege*, *Tsankawi*, *Tyuonyi*, and *Puye* to the Santa Fe Corwith coach yard right around noontime. The six took their places easily and virtually unnoticed beside already roadwise lightweight sisters on the *Chiefs* and three waiting Budd cars, *Agathla*, *Awatobi*, and *San Clemente*, which had come into town the day before on the last run of *Super-2½*.

After lunch on that hot July day, the six P-S newcomers, bearings checked or packed, air-lines inspected, brake-shoes and cylinders gone over, and dozens of other items scrutinized, fell-in behind a sporty, lightly-steaming "Pacific" and, with their new wheels clicking and pinging softly over the rail joints, puffed away from Corwith.

Out onto the "Main," and gathering momentum by the second, they went for a speedy shakedown run to Chillicothe, submitting to all sorts of braking tests, whip-lashing accelerations, and anything else that Santa Fe's men chose to put them through to shake, rattle, and roll and/or unhinge Pullman-Standard's recent labors. Oldtimers who were on-board her for that speed-test and now-grizzled bystanders who watched her zip by tell how observation car *Puye's* "tail" flipped so sharply in-and-out of curves she looked like a "burleycue dancer finishing her act at the old Gaiety Theatre in Chicago."

Tested, tried, and tortured, perspiring freely from every moving part, the *Super-3* "six" made a heated re-entry into Corwith, shed their barely-winded "Pacific" and exhaled hotly ... "passed" for mainline duty the next day.

July 2nd dawned with all the symptoms of a scorcher in Chicago. A few vestiges of night air lingered but, by sun-up, the rays were orangey and hard-at-work! The glare tinted everything in Corwith Yard and the Celcius was climbing fast. The sun was reflected in the fluted sides of the six new *Super-3* cars like a myriad of egg yolks, and it wasn't long 'til it had heated those sides and set them to creaking from the dissipation of the pre-dawn cooling. During the night, the yard crews had strung together the first *Super-3*—all the cars that were made for it—and put them on Track 4. It wasn't really an unusual sight as they greeted the morning but, all the same, the "pieces" were, at last, where they belonged.

Stocking *The Super Chief, Super-3* specifically, as the reader is by now well aware, followed set patterns and, that hot morning, just as it had on other *Supers,* concluded in time to "meet" its switch engine and back-up to the depot. They set her on Track 5 and, like a hundred-and-some-times previously, she settled down to await her patrons. The trainshed radiated with late afternoon heat waves and the air was heavy, cinder-laden, and worst of all, caused one's clothes to stick to the skin. It had indeed been a scorcher, and it was still two hours 'til sunset!

Shadows were lengthening by the time they opened the gates for *Super-3* and the mugginess was subsiding somewhat, but you would have had a hard time convincing the red caps that that was so—particularly the stout one who was leading Bob Burns—the ol' Arkansas Traveler—toward his Pullman, all but weighted down with five pigskin bags, antiquated, label-spattered, and battered from years of vaudeville journeying.

The putty-nosed Burns, in an ill-fitting seersucker suit with a corn-cob pipe tucked in the corner of his mouth, was lugging, gingerly it seemed, an odd-shaped case that held his cherished, homemade solo instrument, "The Bazooka" (two lengths of pipe

Super-3 spins through the yards outside Chicago, as it races to keep its on-time performance. — PAUL STRINGHAM

and a funnel worked by a wire, trombone-like, to produce an asthmatic, tremulous bass tone).

Burns enlivened the unspeakable drabness of the Dearborn shed just by entering it. He trotted rather than walked through the gate and knitted his brows with lovable severity. He and his burdened red cap climbed, with obvious relief, into the air-conditioned sanctuary of *Tyuonyi* and there, in Compartment "B," the Ozark comic of the old Bing Crosby-Kraft Music Hall slumped into a seat and took a healthy pull on a pint of sour mash which he produced from an inside coat pocket.

Palming the cork back into his downhome "squeezin's," the beefy radio rustic pressed a bill in the "cap's" hand, followed him out into the corridor, and then moseyed back to the next car, *Puye,* and on into the dim coolness of the coppery, turquoise, blanket-patterned lounge. Taking a chair at the far end of the lounge, he unwound his big, dishevelled frame and turned his head to stare out the rear window—a spot from which he could watch the perspiring crowd hurrying to get aboard.

Burns crossed his long legs (revealing a happy incongruity of red French lisle socks), breathed-in the cool conditioned air, and

231

Puye

Brand new *Puye* — Pullman-Standard's 4-Drawing Room and 1-Double Bedroom Observation Lounge car for *Super Chief-3* — pristinely stands for the company cameraman at the Pullman-Standard plant in South Chicago. Remarkably imitative, the car's observation lounge so closely approximated its Budd-built predecessor, *Navajo*, that it startled first-viewers. Closer inspection of the interior, as shown on the opposite page, did reveal *decor* differences such as Venetian blinds instead of shades and drapes, cove-lighted ceiling rather than an unlighted vault, plain deep blue arm chairs at the rounded *galleria*, lamps on the magazine racks, and a round-windowed door. In *Puye's* Indian lounge room, Pullman-Standard did, indeed, turn out one of the most charming and striking examples of car building in its long sequence of manufacturing.
—ALL PULLMAN-STANDARD

thrust a big hand back into his inside coat pocket. Pure comfort!

As long as we're "in" the *Puye* lounge with the relaxing Burns, suppose we take a few more moments and highlight that most unique room on a Pullman car. *Puye's* chief claim to uniqueness lay in the fact that it was the one time in their long history that Pullman-Standard ever copied—not "cold" but awfully close— part of a car built by another car-builder ... namely the Budd-built observation car *Navajo* (and *Navajo,* it's worth adding, was the one and only sleeper-observation car that Budd ever built for Santa Fe).

Basic P-S structure configuration prevented *Puye's* observation area from being an exact copy of the one in *Navajo,* but as we've said, it was close enough so that the majority of *Super* riders didn't and maybe never would know the difference. No doubt few of them cared ... and still don't. However, the author and a handful of staunch train *devotées* ... ah, they detected the subtle variances in things of the *Puye* lounge.

Things like the soffited lighting beneath the vaulted ceiling, the placement and sizes of the windows, Venetian blinds instead of window shades, smooth rather than rough backgrounds in the "sand paintings" between the windows, the door and its circular window that led out into the corridor, a bulkier writing desk and bookcase beside it, no table or goatskin-shaded silver lamp at the end window but four deep bluish-purple armchairs in their place. Subtle yet pronounced differences.

Even on the outside of *Puye,* P-S attempted to imitate. Under the very end window, they recessed the frame of the circular "Super Chief" sign into the wall, not as deeply as the one on *Navajo,* but again, almost.

So then, July 2nd, 1938 ... there she was—*Super-3*—all lined up and ready to go, the other half of a "dynamic duo" that would ply, back and forth, between Chicago and the Coast without respite or replacement for the next ten-years. She would run prestigiously and profitably throughout the remainder of the Thirties and up into the early Forties. Other adventures of varying degrees of magnitude awaited her but ... that comes later, in other volumes.

"7:15" and, with Bob Burns still ensconced in the curved "tail" of *Puye* (perhaps a little more mellow by then), *Super-3* flowed out of Dearborn, snaked into the reddening sun, and was off on its first run to "Hollywood."

21

T'was the night before Christmas" of '38 and "all through" drafty Dearborn depot, a *lot* of "creatures" were "stirring!"—stirring out of taxis, stomping snow from their shoes out in the waiting room and, most importantly to them, fleeing the howling, icy winds off Lake Michigan by taking refuge in the incandescent warmth of the cars on *Super-3*.

That Saturday night—the mercury hovering near zero—was just made for snuggling down in a stateroom window-seat or, better still, burrowing deep beneath the blankets of a toasty berth ... icy snowflakes pecking against the window, the wheels clicking softly and, best of all, the muted blurt of the air horn filtering back, waveringly, from the Diesel engines.

Before sleep, however, there were Christmas Eve things to see and do, for *Super-3* was aglow with Yuletide colors and smells. The scent of pinebough corsages and sprigs of holly in the gentlemen's hat-bands mingled with the wet mustiness of fur coats and the woody tang of sawdust that the passengers had gotten on their shoes walking through the layer of it laid down inside the entryway to keep people from slipping. The not unusual cloy of grain-alcohol lent its distilled musk to things. Similarly, m'lady's winter fragrances of *Giulistanari* and *Mon Ange* piquantly accented the heated car air along with smoky gusts from "Rhumba Club" and "El Pasticcio" Havana cigars.

Pullman-Standard *Puye* carries the observation end of *Super-3* and is about to be swallowed up by one of the twin-tunnels at Wootton, summit of Raton Pass, on December 26, 1938. — OTTO PERRY

Bette Davis, the clips of her galoshes clinking a merry, metallic cadence, swung past the length of *Puye,* mounted its steps, and shouldered briskly through the door and on into Bedroom "A." Inside, she plopped a red hat-bag on the russet carpet and the latest *Harper's* and *Vogue* onto the matching seat. She was no sooner settled-in than Bradshaw Crandell, the illustrator, poked his head in the door, causing her to cough-up an inhalation of cigarette smoke. Crandell had pasteled her portrait for a *Cosmopolitan* cover earlier in the year, and his "Hello, Jezebel" caught her quite off-guard.

Further aft, out of Drawing Room "D," John Barrymore, a dashing and dandy old hand at *Super Chiefery,* strode stagily back to the Indian lounge, and "what to his wondering eyes should appear but" cozy *Puye* all done-up as a vision of Yuletide spirit.

Leading Barrymore's eyes in from the doorway were garlands of pine boughs strung along the face of the light soffit with pine

236

cones, like tassels, at every garland-point. On each magazine case—atop the reading lamps—were more pine branches, tiny ones, clipped and shaped like Christmas-tree tops ... softly lighted from underneath by the lamps' bulbs. Over the end window hung a luxuriant fir wreath with a brilliant turquoise velvet ribbon-and-bow instead of the customary red one. The small bulbs up in the soffit reflected in the turquoise lacquered ceiling and looked very much like "strings" of blue lights.

Platters of fresh-baked cookies and cakes nestled under the twin "trees"—an inviting array of goodies iced with bits of red and green and dustings of powdered sugar. Bowls of fat pecans and glistening salted almonds vied for attention with the sweet-cakes. Christmas was rarely Christmasier than it was that night in *Puye*!

Super-3 is just leaving Pasadena, bound for the new Los Angeles Union Station, when this photograph was taken in early 1940. No. 13A and B had only been received from the Electro-Motive Division of General Motors a few weeks earlier. — FRANK PETERSON

Just as there were in *Puye,* platters of all kinds of nuts—fresh and hot from diner ovens—stood, buttered and salted, on the cocktail-tables and atop the bar in the lounge car, *Agathla.* Christmas carols drifted from the Indian-emblemed radio-speaker to fill the warm lounge with their haunting, ancient melodies and, outside the windows, steam vapor trailed-up past them like ghostly wisps of shredded cotton.

Aboard the resplendent diner *Awatobi,* everything was ready for "The Night Before Christmas" guests. In the hot confines of his kitchen, looking like something out of a Leyendecker painting, red-faced chef Baccio Bandinelli and his aides were moving swiftly, back and forth, before their steaming ranges and ovens . . . muscling heavy pans on and in them. The clatter-and-bang had a homey ring to it and made the prospect of dinner all the more tempting.

The moment one merely opened the door to *Awatobi,* unsuspecting nostrils tingled with the foresty tang of the pine branches that hung everywhere—that and the aroma of anise and molasses in the displays of cookies set-out, here and there, in dishes and platters. Along with the smells of Christmas, the tastes of Christmas were sweetly imminent.

With everyone tucked-in, so to speak, Christmas lights twinkling, turkeys roasting, egg-nogs gentling, *Super-3* lifted her skirts, sighed airily, and edged gamely out into the snowy night.

At the same time *Super-3* was departing Chicago on Christmas Eve Saturday, 1938, out in the dark, freezing mountain-snows of New Mexico, near a town called Nolan, *Super-2* was working her way eastward, her staterooms packed with holiday-riders, many of whom were at-dinner in *Cochiti—Cochiti,* where the mahogany walls were cheerily "decked" with pine branches, holly, and tufts of desert berries, all of them fastened with red-and-white beaded straps made by Navajo craftsmen. Hanging over the face of the peach-colored buffet-mirror was an enormous "Delarobia" wreath done by youngsters back in Los Angeles. Beaming steward Peter Tausch even wore a fragrant puff of greasewood leaves in his lapel and proffered menus printed in holiday reds and greens.

The white linen-draped tables bore pots of the richest, reddest poinsettias and, as on *Super-3,* creamy egg-nogs floated in frosty pewter mugs topped with bits of mint and holly leaves. Since *Super-2* would arrive in Chicago Christmas Day around noon and would therefore not serve dinner, *that* Saturday night—the 24th—was "Christmas Dinner," and the folk at Fred Harvey omitted nothing in the way of bounty and brilliance in *Cochiti's* Dickensian setting.

Luscious, fat-breasted turkeys, crisply and luminously browned, were hauled, steaming, from the kitchen, ringed with ruby red cranberries and again, holly leaves. There were all the fixin's: cumulus clouds of mashed potatoes dotted with sunny chunks of melting butter, heaping bowlsful of sagey-savory dressing, corn cooked Indian style, watermelon rind pickles, relishes and peppers, ethereal hot biscuits, spicy pumpkin pie with finger-dented crust edgings, and pots and pots of rich, dark coffee.

In the lounge car, a sprightly Christmas tree stood like a little lighted sentinel at the end of the bar, and a festoonery of pine boughs trailed along over the tan-draped windows.

Back in the observation lounge of *Navajo*, clusters of smoke tree and ironwood branches—hung with shiny sleigh bells—sat on the magazine tables to greet the eyes of pre-dinner loungers, who nibbled eagerly on roasted chestnuts filling two big pewter dishes flanking the silver lamp that graced the ebony-topped end table.

Tausch's "Second Call" for dinner hadn't yet gotten to *Navajo* and the anticipation of it kept a steady procession of the hungry to the chestnut bowls. Just below the ceiling's edge, tiny clear bulbs were strung amongst piñon boughs, and the warmth of the bulbs against the boughs caused their fragrance to permeate the car. Ah, sweet Christmas Eve, and *Super-2* rolled on through the night, Chicago bound. 1938 was drawing to a close.

The *Super Chief* had this new "Spanish-styled" Union Station as its western terminus when the Los Angeles Union Passenger Terminal was opened in July of 1939. The structure created a "fitting" front door for the City of the Angels, but was infinitely less romantic than old La Grande Station. — DONALD DUKE

22

The year 1939 found *The Supers* dashing dutifully between their terminals in sun, rain, snow, sleet, sandstorms, floods, washouts—name it, they went through it. The Broadway and Hollywood crowd kept the cars filled as they drank, dined, dallied, and dreamed their way to appointments, conferences, rehearsals, and productions, set down at their destinations with marvelous regularity and practiced professionalism by Santa Fe. Batting champs and prize fighters, tenors and touts, all got on-board to rub elbows with board chairmen and brokers, politicians and producers, thus keeping the directory-diverse manifests glowing and glittering—a *classe premier* train, building, day by day, *The Super* legend. Santa Fe could not have been happier!

The Depression subsided and the country, right along with *The Super,* made headway. In July of 1939, unappealing as the memory of it strikes the crusty cerebrations of this author, the white-walled Los Angeles Union Passenger Terminal opened and *The Supers,* then, had a new, although infinitely less romantic, western terminus. LAUPT, as it came to be known among the cryptically oriented, telegraphed, as it were, a marked change in *Super Chiefery* just as it did alterations in its namesake city by opening up the gently isolated isolation of the Twenties and Thirties.

The "grand" waiting room of Los Angeles Union Passenger Terminal with its soft leather seats. This scene looks west toward the main entrance. — DONALD DUKE

Trainloads of Easterners, seeking the "golden pavements" of The City of The Angels, pulled into LAUPT barely moments after it opened. They came, those Easterners, to Southern California's palmy confines via "sailing" *Streamliners, Scouts, Challengers, Sunsets, Argonauts,* and in some cases, even *Larks* and *Owls.* But *The Super Chief,* ah, that's the way the vivid and colorful people got to LAUPT and, by their garish and gaudy garb, lent the place its only color, its only real color.

Throughout 1940, a year precious to the author, and for 340-days of 1941, *The Supers* kept right on plying their quite elegant trade between Chicago and Los Angeles—"Hollywood" to those who prefer that terminalizing term—and in the freighting of their non-average patrons, charmed them into becoming regulars of Santa Fe's finest trains. By their inordinately predictable regularity, *The Supers* stood out irregularly.

242

Be assured, though, that it often took above average, way above average performances by their engine crews to make the glove-tight 39-hour and 45-minute schedule. However, there were some great old "runners" handling *The Supers'* throttles in those days and, by George, they took their work seriously. Time was money . . . time was short . . . time was met!

—*Super* CHIEF

The smoothness and predictability of *The Super* program was shattered by two static-filled radio broadcasts on Sunday, December 7th, 1941. *Super-2*, romping along in good reception area about fifty-miles west of Chicago—around 55-minutes after noon—got the word first. The handful of imbibers downing last-minute drinks before arrival in the Windy City were visibly shaken by the announcement that none of them would ever forget. Quite literally, one could have cut the silence with a knife, and the clicking of the wheels lent a peculiarly rhythmic-metallic emphasis to the grim news of Pearl Harbor . . . something like a percussively persistent "what brought this on?"—"what brought this on?"—"what brought this on?"

Super-3 got its Pearl Harbor shock from a message handed up to its conductor as they passed through Otero, New Mexico, above five-miles west of Raton. As it did on its eastbound counterpart, the news also slammed into the solar-plexii of "3's" passengers like body blows, and sent ominous shivers throughout its staterooms and other gathering places—the lounge car especially, since that's where the radio was. As the morning lengthened, the air waves were cluttered with doomsday rhetoric, and one would have had to "color" both the December 7th, 1941 *Supers* pallorous, full lengths of gray, a coloring they would "wear" for three-and-a-half troubled years.

It wasn't long until *The Supers* became a mish-mash of brass, braid, and braggadocio as preferred riders jostled one another for space—any space—on board Nos. 17 and 18. Oak leaves and gold-striped sleeves blossomed amongst *The Supers'* innards like poppies in a field. The higher the rank, the surer that traveller was to wind up in a *Super* berth. It follows that vying for its accommodations became more spirited, almost hand to hand "combat," day by day, trip by trip.

The Hollywooders, the un-uniformed, battled the entrenched military gamely by unlimbering their heaviest weapon, *money.*

Well-heeled producers and directors thought nothing of peeling off twenties and fifties to "sweeten" the regular fare and secure spots—any spots—on *The Supers*. The bidding grew livelier by the minute as both trains readied for departure from Los Angeles and Chicago. It was "war" on *The Supers* as well as on The Front—studied, planned, and plotted! It was every man for himself in the ticket offices, and the devil take the fainthearted! Ante-up and ride; acquiesce and stay home!

The dining cars and lounge cars were alive with war talk and much trafficking in secrets . . . none of which, however, was better kept, more guarded, than the know-how to book space on the next *Super*. And even when two-hours were added to its schedule on July 7th, 1942, competition to ride *The Super* continued unabated; as a matter of fact, more vigorously than ever before.

Wartime was also ego time, and much of *The Supers'* braid-and-brass ridership was merely transplantings from its peacetime passenger lists—passengers who, war or no, would ride no train but *The Super!* So it was business as usual, even better, as World War II dawned for Santa Fe.

With the advent of Pearl Harbor, *The Super Chief* ended one era and began another. Most of us went off to war. The author and *The Super* were separated. A "love affair" was over.

Pleasant Afterthoughts

The early *Super Chief*, at least if one is entirely objective in analyzing her, had a compartmentalized career. Its first year—the six-car, renovated-Pullman months—was 53-round trips of running the gamut from the soul-trying, heart-aching tribulations of Diesel development to the sweet success of setting down happy passengers in Hollywood or Chicago . . . just in time to do the business for which *The Super* was dreamt up and created. 1936–'37 was 236,000-miles of breaking in engines, crews, and cargo—honing an hour-bursting dream schedule to its sharpest edge, making *The Super* all that the word implies.

In that first year, the exclusivity of *The Super Chief* was nowhere more apparent than in the May 10, 1936 Santa Fe timetable, where its equipment-list and the condensation of its schedule were, in this author's opinion, an epic declaration of aristocratic smallness (just six-cars, 79-passengers) and birdlike alightings at the fabled, few-and-far-between outposts of the West. What's more, in 1936 Santa Fe made strategic use of that cherished symbol of uniqueness, the word "only" (stops "Wednesdays only," "Pullmans only").

In other words, with its first, made-at-home *Super Chief*, the forerunner of them all, Santa Fe left no doubt in anyone's mind that it was the *only* train of its kind on their rails. From the very

Low-angle profile of *Super Chief* westbound at Pasadena. With World War-II just around the corner, the *Super* raced a legend into history. — STAN KISTLER

beginning, not just anyone could ride *The Super,* and those who did were, by God, moving in the "high cotton!"

So then, we've delved into, dealt with, investigated, pondered over, and delineated a wide spectrum of compartmentalized pioneer *Super Chiefery* ... from the germination of the idea, to the homemade *Super-1,* to the customizing and publicizing of *Super-2,* to the conglomerate *Super-2½,* to the what-why-and-wherefore of the late blooming *Super-3.* In other words, we have turned the subject of early *Super Chiefing* every way but loose and that, it seems to this writer, should end it. End an ardent lover's reminiscing, nostalgicizing, yes, even agonizing over the great days of a great train ... the great days of *The Super Chief* as he knew them intimately, consistently, and to be sure, lovingly.

The last words of first-hand affection are now done with. The heartwarming recollections have all been spilled onto these pages for any and all who can contemporize, and also for those blessed souls who, even from a distance, lived around *The Super Chief* when, between 1936 and 1941, she raced a legend into history.

For her post-war years, her latter days, let another devoted heart set down the scented memories of those times and may that chronicler be but half as delighted in the doing of it as Stan Repp has been in sharing his great days of *The Super Chief.*

The office of station agent Myer Mendelsohn, at the eastern
perimeter of this enchanting old structure, was a study of castoff
and downcast furniture surrounded by "walls" of celebrity portraits.
Covering the floor was an Oriental rug lacking any kind of
description, stained by coffee and greasy feet over the years.
Mendelsohn moved into the cozy trackside office in 1893 and
occupied the "throne" for 46 years. For nearly a half-century, this
office and the pudgy agent *were* "Santa Fe" in Los Angeles.

Mendelsohn of La Grande

Much to the delight of those of us who frequented them, almost all old train stations boasted at least one intriguing room, whether it was for the riding public or, once in a while, to make it even more fascinating, one that only a scant few had access to.

It was just such a room-for-the-few that B.F. Levet, its designer, tacked onto the eastern perimeter of La Grande Station—a riot of the bricklayer's art that the Santa Fe Railway put up in 1893 at the end of Second Street in Los Angeles. THE room in that altogether enchanting old depot was, from the time it opened, the office of agent Myer Mendelsohn, a classic study in rotundity, nearly a carbon-copy of Mr. Pickwick except that Mendelsohn was a bit more owlish and somewhat chunkier.

Myer was a cigar-lover, a natural greeter, a rail romantic, and a connoisseur of the best and richest coffee-cakes in Southern California. When he moved into his trackside office in '93, Mendelsohn moved in to stay, and stay he did—for forty-six years, nearly a half-century of unrivaled identity as "Mr. Santa Fe" in Los Angeles.

Settling-in with real purpose, Myer wrapped his pudginess within the nubby-plastered walls and ceiling as though they were a cocoon. To cozy-up the place in its chrysalis stage, he assembled an outlandish conglomeration of cast-off and downcast furniture which he capriciously embellished as the years went by.

By 1936, when the author first set foot in it, the room was a veritable hodge-podge of shapes, sizes, and textures, all of them sweetly saturated with forty-three years of good cigar smoke, the aroma of strong coffee, and soft coal dust.

Riding the floor, like something dragged from an itinerant sheik's tent, was an oriental rug of nebulous pattern and questionable ancestry, so stained that its predominant color was "greasy feet."

At the periphery of that disreputable drugget, centered on the east wall, was a big, old roll-top desk, cubbyholed and cluttered, worthy of a Mark Twain or a William Allen White. Before it was an equally aged, badly sprung office chair with a purple pillow stuffed in it, the tassels of which extruded through the arm-rungs like four mauve pitons.

Architect B. Frank Levet's 1893, $30,000 red brick epic, the La Grande Station on Santa Fe Avenue in Los Angeles, was a riot of the mason's art offering up a multiplicity of corbels, corbisteps, dentil cornices, niches, and ogee, saracenic, and trifoliated arches! La Grande — the *Super Chief's* first western terminus — was, under its cloak of ivy, grime and time, *the* most inviting place from which to train-watch and nowhere was the *Super's* poshness more strikingly evident than when she was parked alongside La Grande . . . far more dramatic than what Hollywood could ever have dreamed up. La Grande and *The Super* are both sorely missed — RALPH MELCHING

To the right of the desk and chair stood a '93 varnished wood filing-cabinet, its edges battered and rounded—Myer's "data bank," out of which papers of long-forgotten urgency peeked wrinkledly. Atop the cabinet, in an attempt at keeping matters current, sat a wire basket billowing with mimeographed, typed (all-caps), and hand-written sheets of paper . . . the scripts-and-scrolls for true public relations. Myer could and did relate to the public!

At the port side of Myer's roll-top, wedged between its north end and an ancient wood-filigreed screen door, postured an oak tambour table over which was draped, railroad casually, a yard-and-a-half of mustard green velvet, pock-marked with hot tobacco droppings, bits of sugar icing, and scattered sulphur stains from wooden matches dropped on it by errant switchmen who came in for coffee-and-conversation with "Ol' Myer."

Opposite the desk, almost springless and with tufts of its stuffing peering from random holes in the brown leather hide, was a couch (in those days, we called them "divans") with hollowed-out seats, elbow-dented arms, looking as though it had expelled all the air from its vitals. On either side of the weary divan, like preposterous sentries, were pedestal lamps with flowered, fringed shades and pink silk linings which cast an odd rosy glow over that side of the room, especially eerie on rainy days.

Boldly stationed in front of the divan was a four-foot circle of walnut coffee-table, tile-topped in the best 1920's "Spanish" motif, and weighted with an array of trade magazines, a brass-bound cigar humidor, a bone china cup and saucer, and a scarlet fez reading "Al Malikah, Greeter."

Now, with the room furnitured, we come to the *pièce de résistance* of the place, what it was that set Myer's office at La Grande far above most agents' offices, what it was that lent his digs an inestimable worth and singular hospitality. Occupying all but a few square inches of wall surface was a galaxy of framed eight-by-ten photos of film stars and stage luminaries, numbering in the hundreds, *all* autographed "To Myer." "To Myer—with affectionate regard," "To Myer—with gratitude," "To Myer—with" whatever the signator chose to pen with flourish typical of show folk.

In just one quadrant of that one-of-a-kind photo gallery were the inscribed likenesses of Adolf Menjou (looking coy in a gray fedora), Clara Bow (pertly marcelled, who signed "Your 'It' Girl"), Janet Gaynor and Charlie Farrell (side by side, of course), Marie Dressler, Lew Cody, Charlie Chaplin holding Jackie "The Kid" Coogan in his arms beneath the brass-railed observation platform and *Chief* tail-sign (signed "To Uncle Myer" in Jackie's boyish scrawl), O.O. McIntyre (who penned "Galliopolis huzzas to Myer from Odd"), Samuel Goldwyn, Eleanor Powell (stepping off the original *Super Chief*), Thomas Meighan, The Douglas Fairbankses, Sr. and Jr., Sue Carrol (swirlingly penned in lavender ink "For Darling Myer"), and on a bracketed wall-shelf above stacks of brochures and pocket-timetables, Zane Grey and Gloria Swanson (in cloche hat and furs). Shirley Temple, becurled, be-cuted, but unsmiling, big-eyed out from between Groucho Marx and the darkly suave Rod La Roque (perhaps the nattiest of all the matinee idols).

On and on and on, platooning around Myer's putty-plastered office, in frame after frame, the "Stars of The Silver Screen," "The Broadway Stage," "Coast-to-Coast Radio," and "The Business World" claimed the viewer with sparkling-toothed photographic imagery, a priceless picture record of traveller-and-train when both ruled supreme.

Myer's panorama of eight-by-tens generated a high nostalgic charge and, simultaneously, did a thoroughgoing job of transforming a workaday room into what was almost an acetated shrine to Santa Fe's *Chief* and *Super Chief devotées*, the people whom Myer so ably, so naturally, so knowingly embraced into the Santa Fe fold. His photos were a pictured tribute to a great "guy," a genuine personality, a good friend, that rarest of rarities, a man who truly liked people.

* Cost of *Super Chief-2* *

Car	Description	Cost
3400	30′ R.P.O.-mail storage	$ 53,858.89
3430	Mail-baggage	48,165.91
Isleta	8 sections, 2 comps., 1 DR	74,329.41
Laguna	8 sections, 2 comps., 1 DR	74,329.41
Acoma	Full lounge, bar, barber shop & crew	77,604.83
Cochiti	36-passenger diner	82,787.42
Oraibi	6 bedrooms, 2 DR, 2 comps.	82,509.42
Taos	6 bedrooms, 2 DR, 2 comps.	82,509.42
Navajo	1 bedroom, 2 DR, 3 comps., ob. lounge	85,984.27
	Cost 9 cars	662,078.98
	Cost 7 passenger cars	560,054.18
	Cost 2 Diesel units	279,619.02
	Total cost cars and locomotive	$941,698.00

Biographical Index

Subject Index

Acknowledgments

With the coming of Amtrak on May 1, 1971, the nation and the railroad world lost its first all-Pullman streamlined passenger train designed for diesels — the *Super Chief*. Following my article "The Story of The Super Chief" in the May 1962 issue of *Trains Magazine,* I decided to chronicle the complete account of my favorite train. I am one of the few alive today who was around during the development, inaugural runs, and early operation of the *Super.*

It would be difficult to single out here all those who have assisted in this venture. Nearly all the *Super Chief* pioneers have now taken the train into the sunset, but I have given each participant due credit in the pages of this book.

Extra special gratitude is expressed to Margaret Repp for encouragement, to Juliana Romm and Eleanor Powell for inspiration, to Adelaide Bledsoe Kingman for generosity, to train architect John Harbeson for recollecting, to John Ellsworth of the Santa Fe for patience, and to Paul Laszlo for devotion to the *Super.*

The material in this book is from my collection unless otherwise credited. I am in debt to the following for their generosity in providing illustrative material to enhance the pages of this book. They are: A. E. Barker, Gerald M. Best, E. L. Branson, the DeGolyer Foundation Library, Donald Duke, L. E. Griffith, Graphic House, Mike Iczkowski, Phillips C. Kauke, R. H. Kindig, Stan Kistler, Ernest M. Leo, R. V. Mehlenbeck, Ralph Melching, the Les Merrill Collection, the late Otto Perry, the late Frank Peterson, the Santa Fe Railway, Paul Stringham, *Trains Magazine* Collection, Washington University Archives, and Allen Youell.

Special appreciation is extended to Raymond Spencer for his artistry of Nos. 1 and 1-A at San Bernardino on its first run, and the streamlined *Super* arriving at La Grande depicted on the jacket and title page. Also to Gil Reid for his enlivening ink drawings, and to Mike Iczkowski, for providing the Leland Knickerbocker rendering of the *Super* appearing on the end papers.

To be a book, any story requires a publisher. Donald Duke, publisher of Golden West Books, has done a great deal more than set type, form layouts, and bind paper. He has provided me encouragement, offered his publishing talent, and extended his own knowledge of the Santa Fe Railway and the *Super Chief.*